CW00408933

OXFORD PHOTO DICTIONARY

ANGOL–MAGYAR

Oxford University Press 1992

Oxford University Press
Walton Street, Oxford OX2 6DP

Oxford New York Toronto Madrid Delhi Bombay
Calcutta Madras Karachi Kuala Lumpur
Singapore Hong Kong Tokyo Nairobi Dar es Salaam
Cape Town Melbourne Auckland

and associated companies in
Berlin Ibadan

Oxford and Oxford English are trade marks of Oxford University Press

ISBN 0 19 431378 6

Hungarian edition © Oxford University Press 1992

All rights reserved. No part of this publication may be reproduced, stored in a retrieval system, or transmitted, in any form or by any means, electronic, mechanical, photocopying, recording, or otherwise, without the prior permission of Oxford University Press.

This book is sold subject to the condition that it shall not, by way of trade or otherwise, be lent, re-sold, hired out, or otherwise circulated without the publisher's prior consent in any form of binding or cover other than that in which it is published and without a similar condition including this condition being imposed on the subsequent purchaser.

Editor: Jane Taylor

Printed in Hong Kong

Acknowledgements

Location and studio photography by: Graham Alder, Chris Andrews, Martyn Chillmaid, Nigel Cull, Nick Fogden, Paul Freestone, Gareth Jones, Mark Mason.

The publishers would like to thank the following for permission to reproduce photographs: ABI Caravans Ltd; Allsport (UK) Ltd/B Asset, S Bruty, R Cheyne, T Duffy, S Dunn, J Gichigi, J Hayt, B Hazelton, H Heiderman, J Loubat, A Murrell, J Nicholson, M Powell, P Rondeau, H Stein; Animal Photography/S Thompson, R Willbie; Ardea London Ltd/D Avon, I Beames, L Beames, J Clegg, E Dragesco, M England, J Ferrero, K Fink, D Greenslade, A Lindau, J Mason, E Mickleburgh, P Morris, S Roberts, R & V Taylor, A Weaving, W Weisser; Art Directors Photo Library/S Grant; Associated Sports Photography; Clive Barda; Barnaby's Picture Library; J Allan Cash Ltd; Bruce Coleman Ltd/J Anthony, E & B Bauer, J Burton, M Dohrn, J Foot, N Fox-Davies, M Kahl, G Langsbury, W Layer, G McCarthy, M Price, A Purcell, H Reinhard, K Taylor, N Tomalin, R Wilmshurst; Colorsport/Compoint; Cotswold Wildlife Park; Cunard Line Ltd; Mary Evans Picture Library; Fiat Fork Lift Trucks; Michael Fogden; Ford Motor Company Ltd; Robert Harding Picture Library/Griffiths, G Renner; Eric Hoskin/W Pitt; Hovertravel Ltd; Libby Howells; The Hutchison Library/M Scorer; Rob Judges; Landscape Only; Frank Lane Picture Agency/A Albinger, R Jones, Silvestris, M Thomas, L West; Leyland Daf; London Tourist Board; Mazda Cars (UK) Ltd; Metropolitan Police; National Motor Museum, Beaulieu; Oxford Scientific Films Stills/S Dalton, L Lauber, M Leach, Partridge Films Ltd, Presstige Pictures, R Redfern, F Skibbe, G Wren; Planet Earth Pictures/Seaphot/M Clay, W Deas, D George, J George, K Lucas, J Lythgoe, N Middleton, J Scott, J Watt; Renault UK Ltd; Rex Features Ltd/N Jorgensen, J Tarrant; Rover Cars; RSPB/G Downey, P Perfect, M Richards; Science Photo Library/T Beddow, M Bond, Dr J Burgess, D Campione, M Dohrn, T Fearon-Jones, V Fleming, NASA, S Patel, R Royer, St Bartholomew's Hospital, J Sanford, S Stammers, J Stevenson, S Terry; Shell UK Ltd; Spectrum Colour Library; Swift Picture Library/T Dressler, M Mockler; Toleman Automotive Ltd; Trust House Forte; Wedgewood; World Pictures; Zefa/D Cattani, Damm, D Davies, Goebel, C Krebs, R Maylander, K Oster, J Pfaff, A Roberts, Rosenfeld, Selitsch.

The publishers would like to thank the following for their help and assistance: Abingdon Hospital; Abingdon Surgery; Russell Acott Ltd; Apollo Theatre; B & L Mechanical Services, Eynsham; Douglas Bader Sports Centre, St Edward's School; Barclays Bank; BBC Radio Oxford; The Bear & Ragged Staff, Cumnor; H C Biggers, Eynsham; Boswells of Oxford; Bournemouth International Airport; British Rail; Cassington Builders Ltd; Cheney School; Cherwell School; City Camera Exchange, Brighton; Comet; Daisies, Oxford; Early Learning Centre; Education & Sci Products Ltd; Elmer Cotton Sports, Oxford; Eynsham Car Repairs; Faulkner & Sons Ltd; For Eyes; Phylis Goodman Ltd, Eynsham; Habitat Designs Ltd; W R Hammond & Son Ltd, Eynsham; Hartford Motors Ltd; Headington Sports; Heather's Delicatessen, Hove; Hove Delicatessen; Inshape Body Studios Ltd; Johnsons of Oxford; Littlewoods PLC; London Underground Ltd; Malin Farms, Eynsham; P J Meagher, Eynsham; John Menzies Ltd; North Kidlington Primary School; Ocean Village Marina, Marina Developments PLC; Nigel Olesen BDS; Options Hair Studio, Eynsham; Oxford Despatch; Oxford Royal Mail & Post Office Counters; Paramount Sewing Machines; Parkwood Veterinary Group; Payless DIY; Phoenix One & Two; Qualifruit; Red Funnel Isle of Wight Ferries; SS Mary & John School; Southampton Eastleigh Airport; Stanhope Wilkinson Associates, Eynsham; Summertown Travel; Texas Homecare, Oxford; Paul Thomas; Richard Walton, Eynsham; Warlands, Cycle Agents; Welsh National Opera; Western Newsagents, Hove; Chris Yapp Consultants Ltd.

Tartalomjegyzék

Family Relationships page 1

John családja	John's Family
nagyanya	**1** grandmother
nagyapa	**2** grandfather
nagynéni	**3** aunt
nagybácsi	**4** uncle
anya	**5** mother
apa	**6** father
após	**7** father-in-law
anyós	**8** mother-in-law
unokatestvér	**9** cousin
sógor	**10** brother-in-law
nővér/húg	**11** sister
feleség	**12** wife
sógórnő	**13** sister-in-law
unokahúg	**14** niece
unokaöccs	**15** nephew
fia	**16** son
lánya	**17** daughter

John Anna **férje**.	**18**	John is Ann's **husband**.
Tom és Lisa Johnnak és Annának a **gyerekei**.	**19**	Tom and Lisa are John and Ann's **children**.
John és Anna Tomnak és Lisának a **szülei**.	**20**	John and Ann are Tom and Lisa's **parents**.
Mary és Bob Cox, valamint Ian és Jane Hill Tomnak és Lisának a **nagyszülei**.	**21**	Mary and Bob Cox and Ian and Jane Hill are Tom and Lisa's **grandparents**.
Tom a **fiúunokájuk**.	**22**	Tom is their **grandson**.
Lisa a **lányunokájuk**.	**23**	Lisa is their **granddaughter**.

Family Relationships

1
Helen Jones
2
Andrew Jones
1
Joan Cox
2
Alan Cox
3
Sally Jones
4
David Jones
3
Jill Jones
5
Mary Cox
6
Bob Cox
7
Ian Hill
8
Jane Hill
9
Rita Jones
9
Sam Jones
10
Paul Day
11
Tina Day
John Cox
12
Ann Cox
13
Carol King
10
Joe King
14
Lucy Day
15
Nick Day
16
Tom Cox
17
Lisa Cox
15
Mark King
14
Sue King

The Human Body 1

page 3

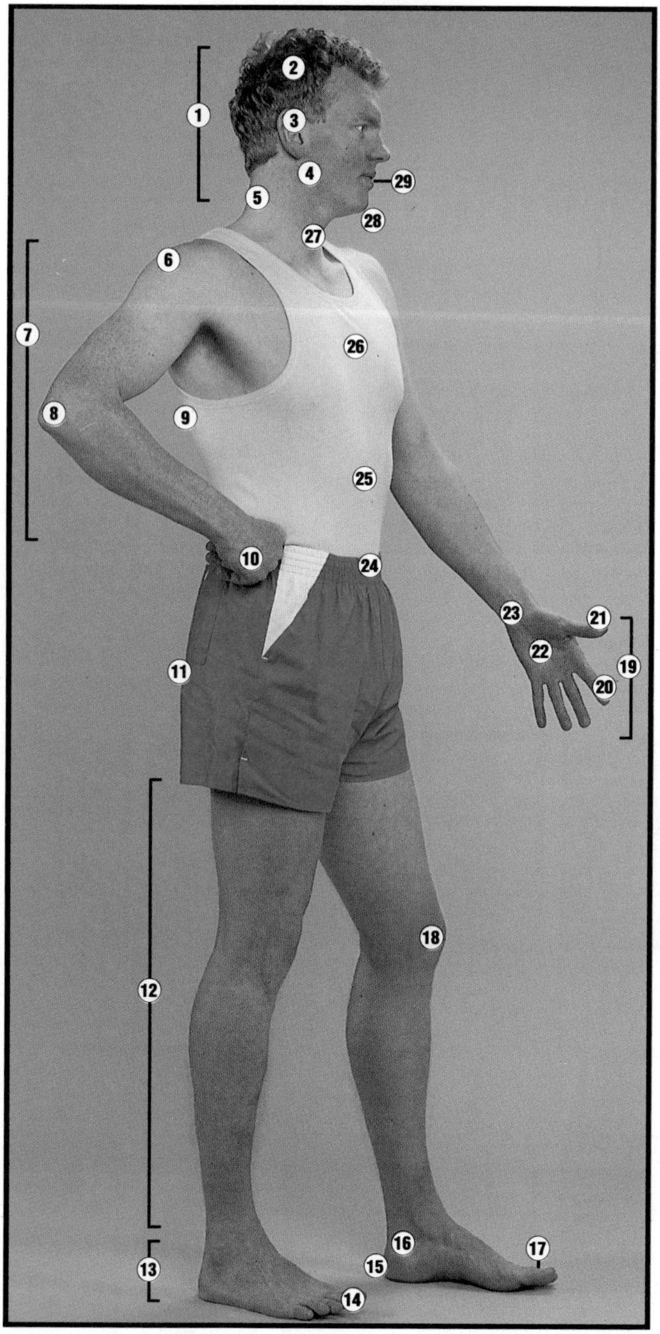

1
2
3
4
5
6
7
8
9
10
11
12
13
14
15
16
17
18
19
20
21
22
23
24
25
26
27
28
29

fej	**1**	head
haj	**2**	hair
fül	**3**	ear
állkapocs	**4**	jaw
nyak	**5**	neck
váll	**6**	shoulder
kar	**7**	arm
könyök	**8**	elbow
hát	**9**	back
ököl	**10**	fist
fenék/ülep	**11**	buttocks/bottom
láb	**12**	leg
lábfej	**13**	foot
lábujj	**14**	toe
sarok	**15**	heel
boka	**16**	ankle
köröm	**17**	nail
térd	**18**	knee
kéz	**19**	hand
(kéz)ujj	**20**	finger
hüvelykujj	**21**	thumb
tenyér	**22**	palm
csukló	**23**	wrist
derék	**24**	waist
has	**25**	stomach
mellkas	**26**	chest
torok	**27**	throat
áll	**28**	chin
száj	**29**	mouth

The Human Body 2

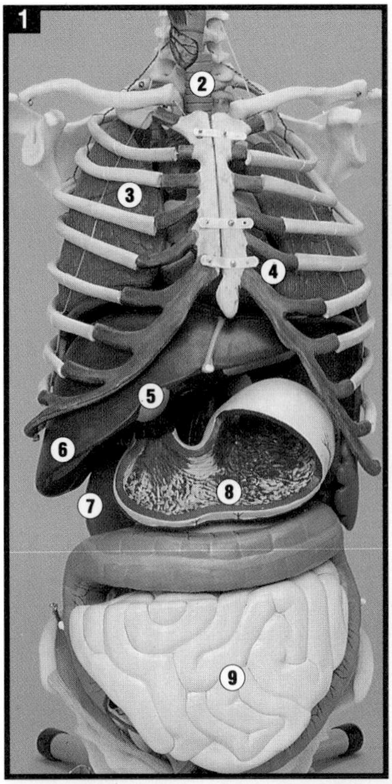
1
2
3
4
5
6
7
8
9

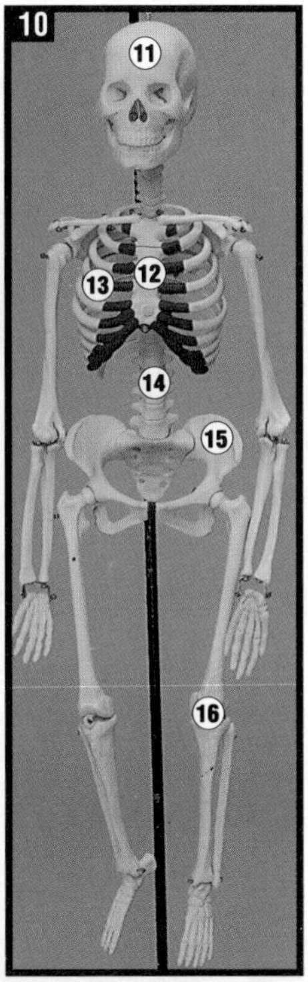
10
11
12
13
14
15
16

belső szervek	**1** internal organs
légcső	**2** trachea/windpipe
tüdő	**3** lung
szív	**4** heart
epehólyag	**5** gall-bladder
máj	**6** liver
vese	**7** kidney
gyomor	**8** stomach
bélrendszer	**9** intestines
csontváz	**10** skeleton
koponya	**11** skull
mellcsont	**12** breastbone
borda	**13** rib
hátgerinc/gerincoszlop	**14** spine/backbone
medencecsont	**15** pelvis/hip-bone
térdkalács	**16** kneecap

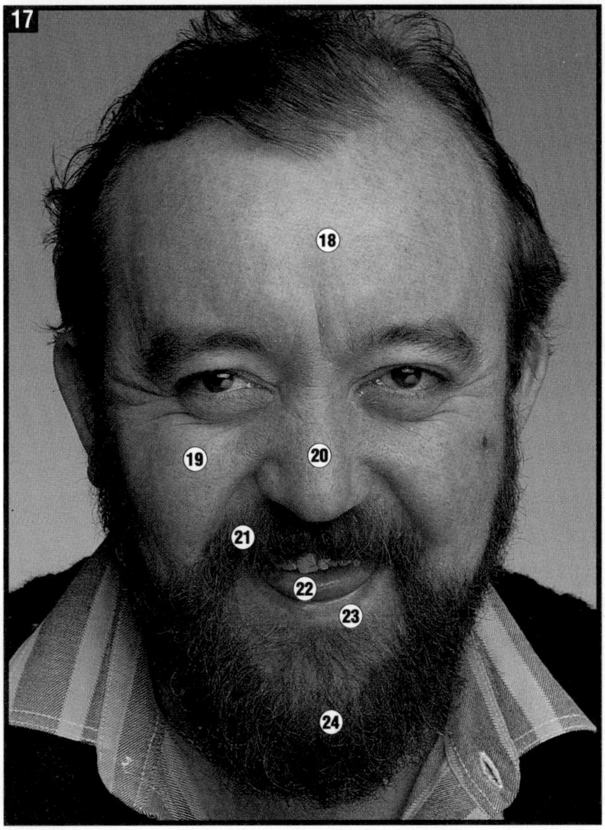
17
18
19
20
21
22
23
24

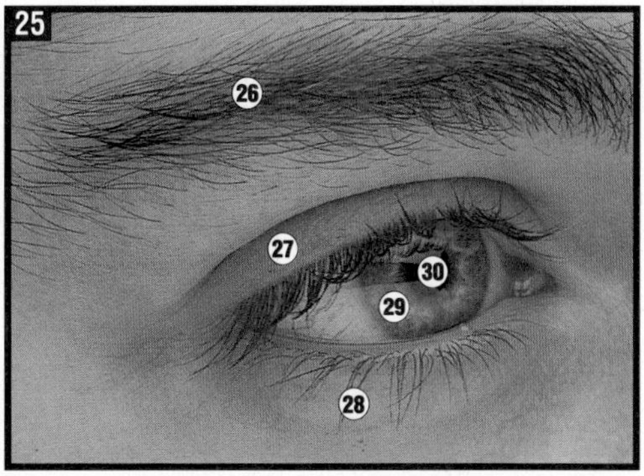
25
26
27
28
29
30

arc	**17** face
homlok	**18** forehead
orca	**19** cheek
orr	**20** nose
bajusz	**21** moustache
nyelv	**22** tongue
ajak	**23** lip
szakáll	**24** beard
szem	**25** eye
szemöldök	**26** eyebrow
szemhéj	**27** eyelid
szempilla	**28** eyelash
szivárványhártya	**29** iris
pupilla	**30** pupil

Physical Description

page 5

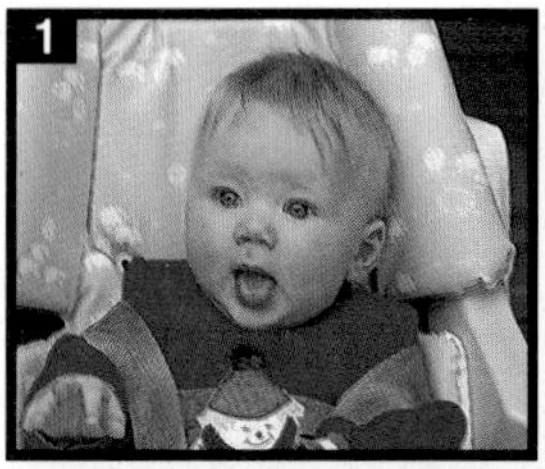
1

2

3

4

5

6
7

8

9

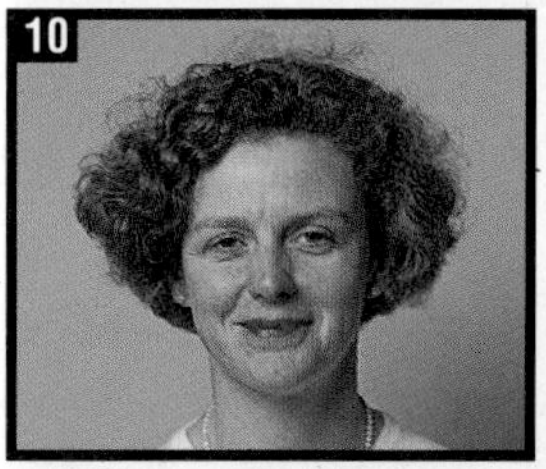
10

11

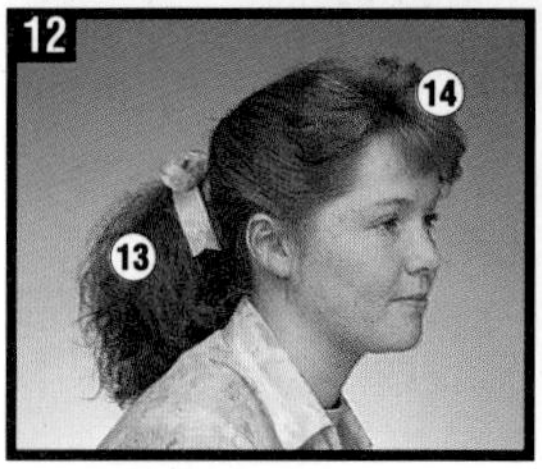
12
14
13

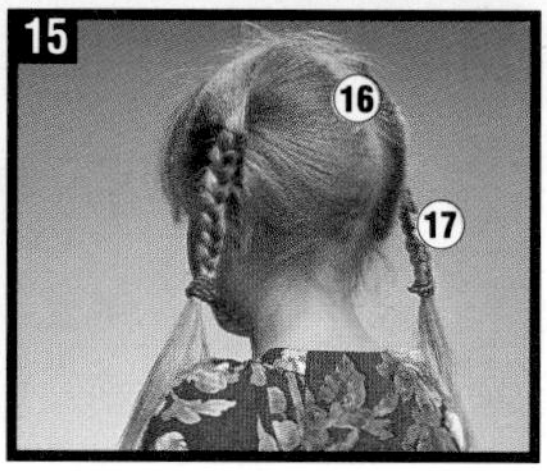
15
16
17

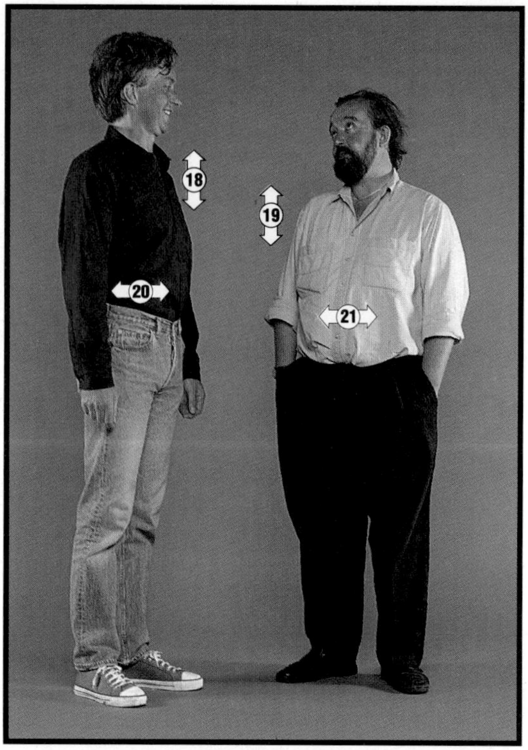
18
19
20
21

Életkor	**Age**
csecsemő	**1** baby
gyerek/kisfiú	**2** child/(young) boy
tizenéves/tizenéves lány	**3** teenager/teenage girl
felnőtt/nő	**4** adult/woman
felnőtt/férfi	**5** adult/man
idősebb (*vagy* öreg) férfi	**6** elderly (*or* old) man
Haj	**Hair**
kopasz fej	**7** bald head
rövid, sima, sötét	**8** short straight dark
rövid, sima, világos	**9** short straight fair
rövid, göndör	**10** short curly
rövid, hullámos	**11** short wavy
hosszú, vörös	**12** long red (*Brit also* ginger)
lófarok	**13** pony tail
frufru	**14** fringe (*US* bangs)
hosszú, szőke	**15** long blonde
választék	**16** parting (*US* part)
hajfonat/copf	**17** plait (*US* braid)
magas	**18** tall
alacsony	**19** short
sovány	**20** thin
kövér	**21** fat

What's the matter?

page 6

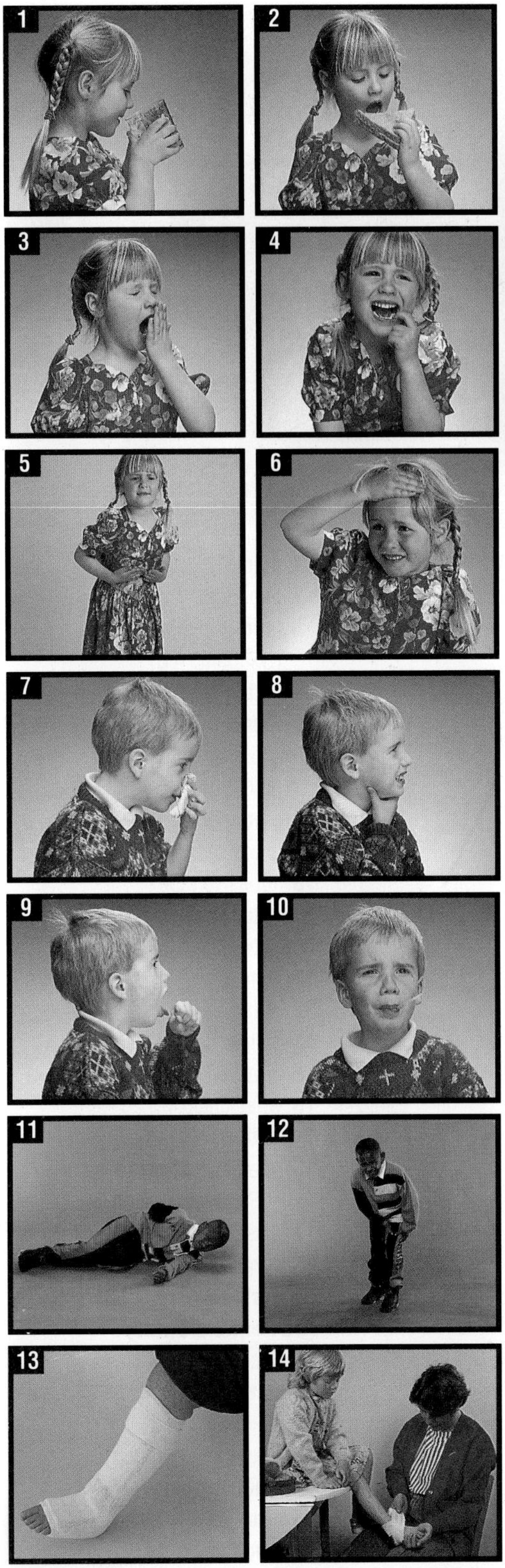

1
2
3
4
5
6
7
8
9
10
11
12
13
14

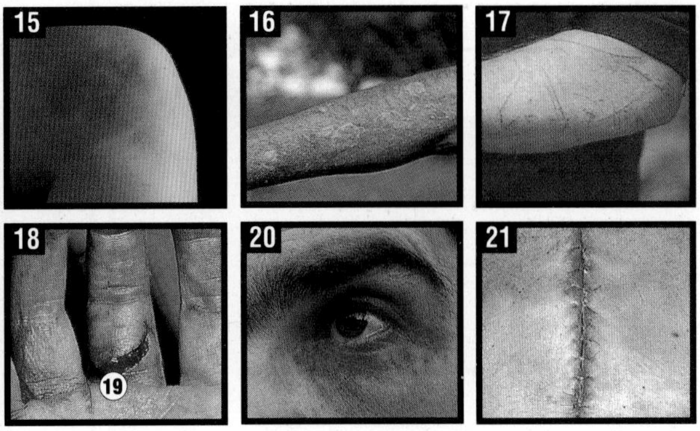

15
16
17
18
19
20
21

Szomjas.	**1** She's thirsty.
Éhes.	**2** She's hungry.
Fáradt.	**3** She's tired.
Fáj a foga.	**4** She's got toothache. (*US* She has a toothache.)
Fáj a gyomra.	**5** She's got stomach-ache. (*US* She has a stomachache.)
Fáj a feje.	**6** She's got a headache. (*US* She has a headache.)
Megfázott.	**7** He's got a cold. (*US* He has a cold.)
Fáj a torka.	**8** He's got a sore throat. (*US* He has a sore throat.)
Köhög.	**9** He's got a cough. (*US* He has a cough.)
Lázas.	**10** He's got a temperature. (*US* He has a temperature.)
Balesetek	**Accidents**
Elesett.	**11** He's fallen over. (*US* He fell over.)
Megütötte a lábát.	**12** He's hurt his leg. (*US* He hurt his leg.)
Eltörte a lábát.	**13** She's broken her leg. (*US* She broke her leg.)
Kificamította a bokáját.	**14** She's sprained her ankle. (*US* She sprained her ankle.)
véraláfutás	**15** bruise
leégés	**16** sunburn
horzsolás	**17** scratch
vágás	**18** cut
vér	**19** blood
(fekete) monokli	**20** black eye
forradás	**21** scar

Health Care 1 page 7

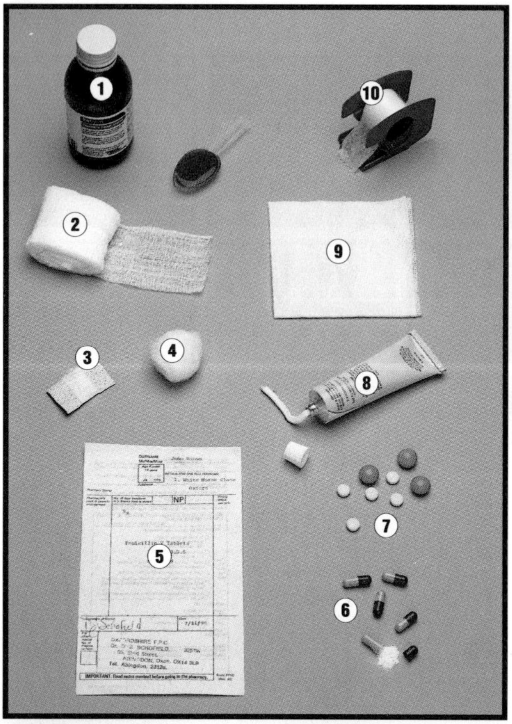
1
2
3
4
5
6
7
8
9
10
NP

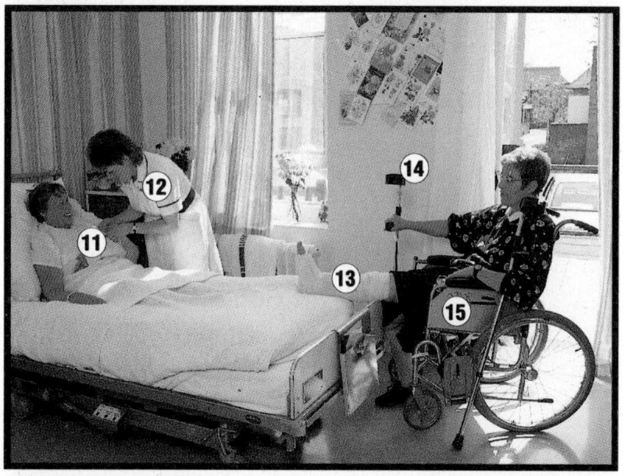
11
12
13
14
15

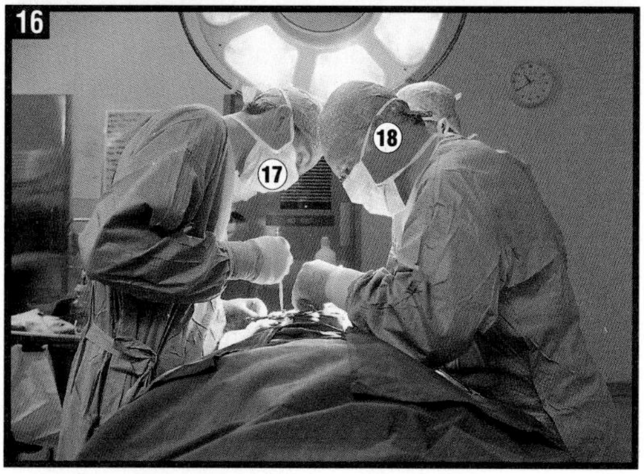
16
17
18

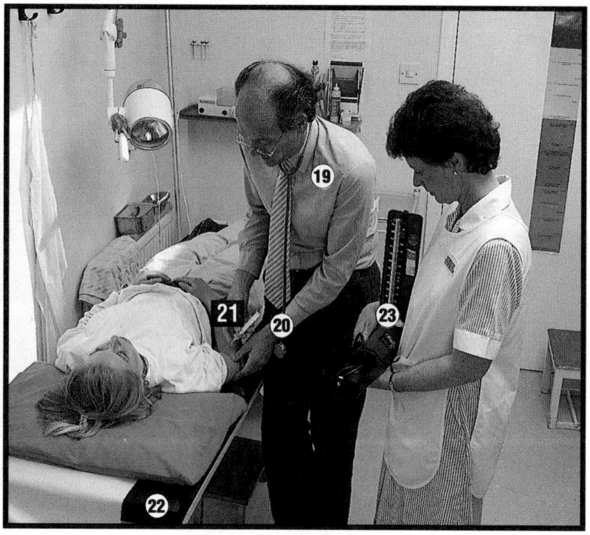
19
20
21
22
23

gyógyszer **1** medicine
kötszer **2** bandage
gyorstapasz **3** (sticking-)plaster (*US* Band-Aid)
vatta **4** cotton wool (*US* cotton ball)
recept **5** prescription
kapszula **6** capsule
tabletta **7** pill/tablet
kenőcs **8** ointment
gézpárna **9** gauze pad
ragtapasz **10** adhesive tape

Kórterem **Hospital Ward (*US also* Hospital Room)**

karfelkötő kendő **11** sling
nővér/ápolónő **12** nurse
gipszkötés **13** plaster cast (*US* cast)
mankó **14** crutch
tolószék **15** wheelchair

Műtét **Operation**

műtő **16** operating theatre (*US* operating room)
maszk **17** mask
sebész **18** surgeon

Orvosi rendelő **Doctor's Surgery (*US* Doctor's Office)**

orvos **19** doctor
szívhallgató **20** stethoscope
injekció **21** injection
vizsgálóasztal **22** examination couch (*US* examining table/ examination table)
vérnyomásmérő készülék **23** blood pressure gauge

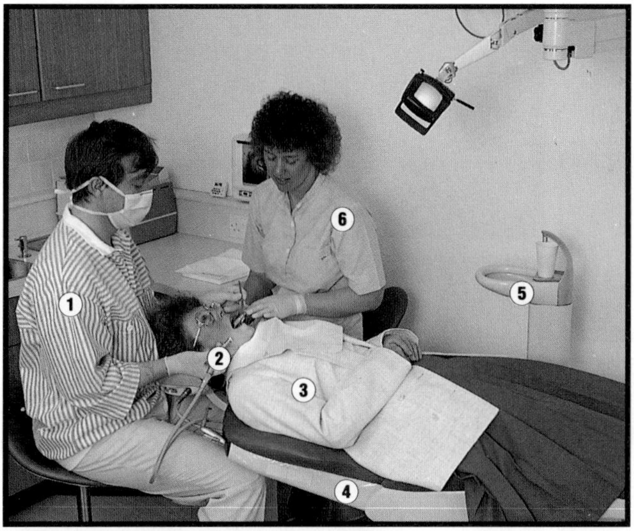
1
2
3
4
5
6

Health Care 2

A fogorvosnál	At the Dentist's
fogorvos	**1** dentist
fúró	**2** drill
beteg	**3** patient
fogorvosi szék	**4** dentist's chair
(öblítő) kagyló	**5** basin
fogászati asszisztens	**6** dental nurse (*US* dental assistant)
íny	**7** gum
fog	**8** tooth
tömés	**9** filling
röntgenfelvétel	**10** X-ray (*also* x-ray)
elülső fogak	**11** front teeth
hátsó fogak	**12** back teeth

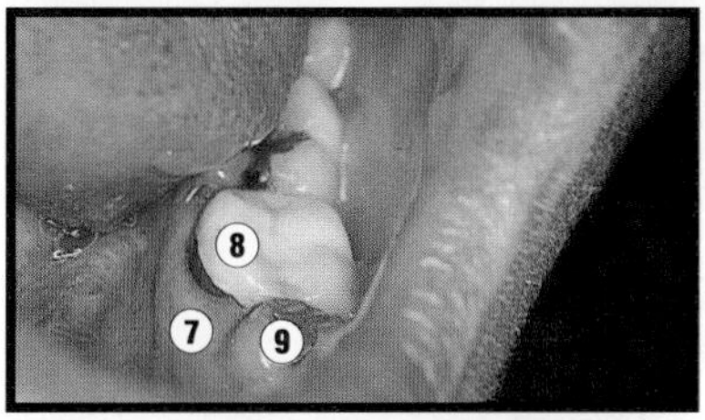
8
7
9

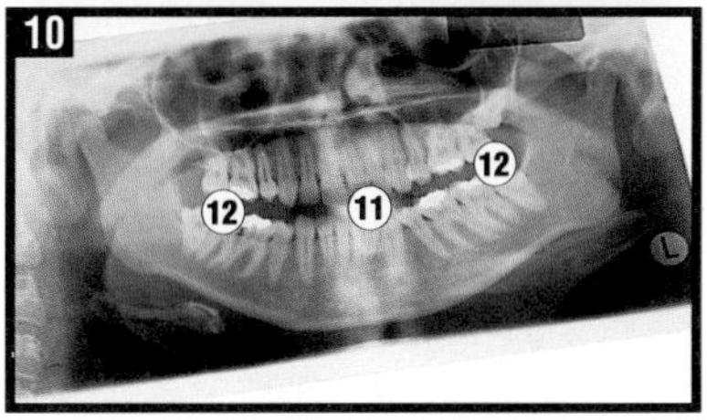
10
12
11
12

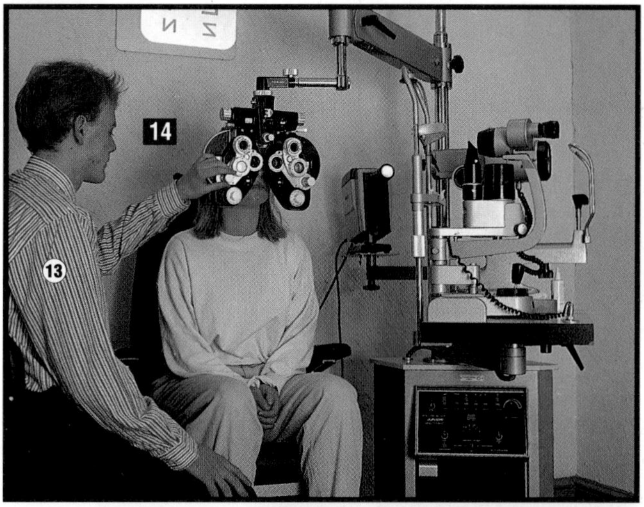
14
13

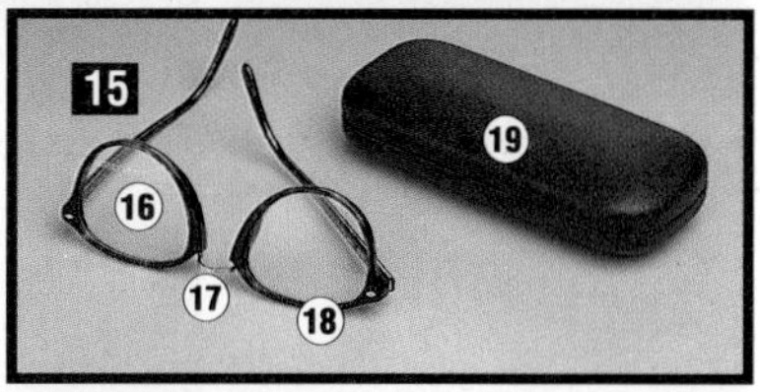
15
16
17
18
19

Az optikusnál	At the Optician's
optikus	**13** optician
szemvizsgálat	**14** eye test
szemüveg	**15** (pair of) glasses
lencse	**16** lens
nyereg	**17** bridge
keret	**18** frame
szemüvegtok	**19** glasses case (*US also* eyeglass case)
kontaktlencse	**20** contact lens
szemcsepp	**21** eye drops
kontaktlencse-tisztító	**22** contact lens cleaner

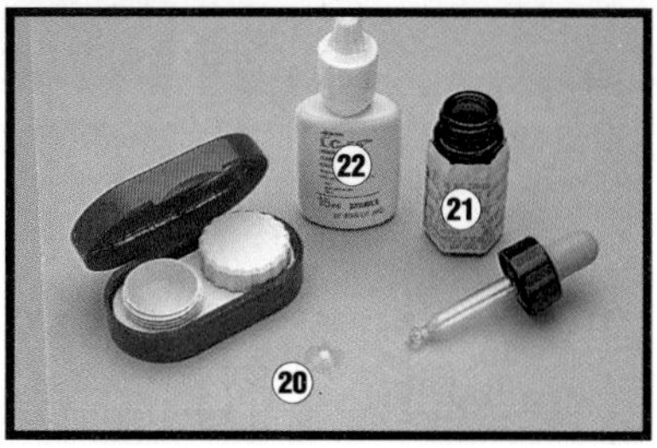
22
21
20

Describing Clothes

page 9

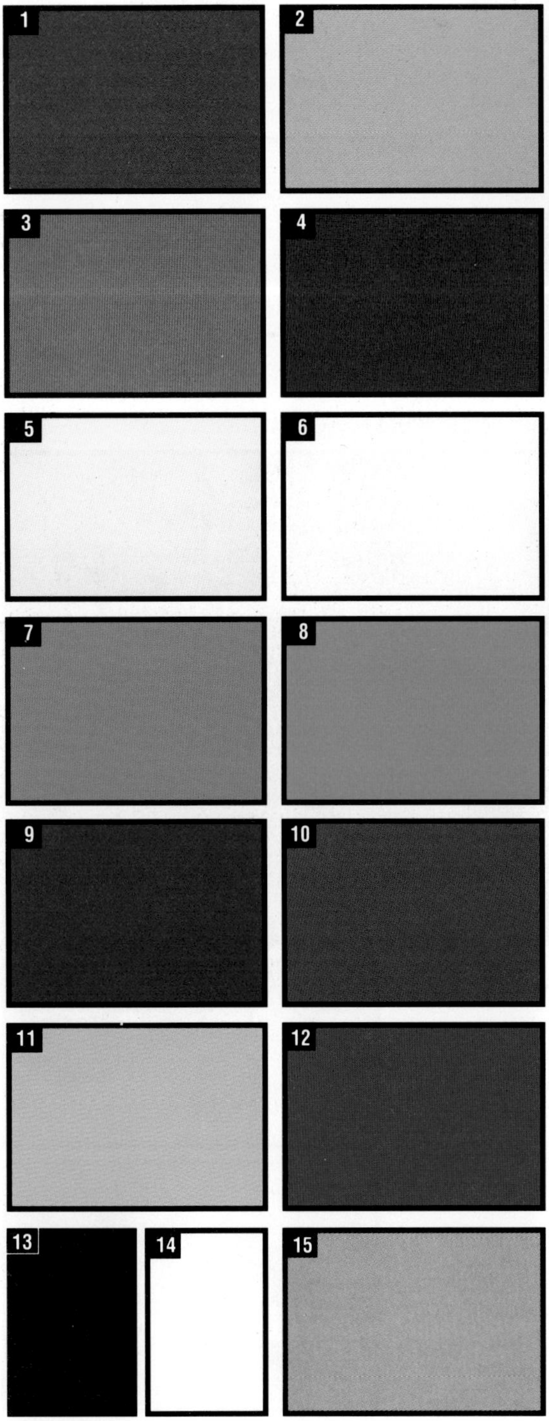
1
2
3
4
5
6
7
8
9
10
11
12
13
14
15

16
17
18
19
20
21

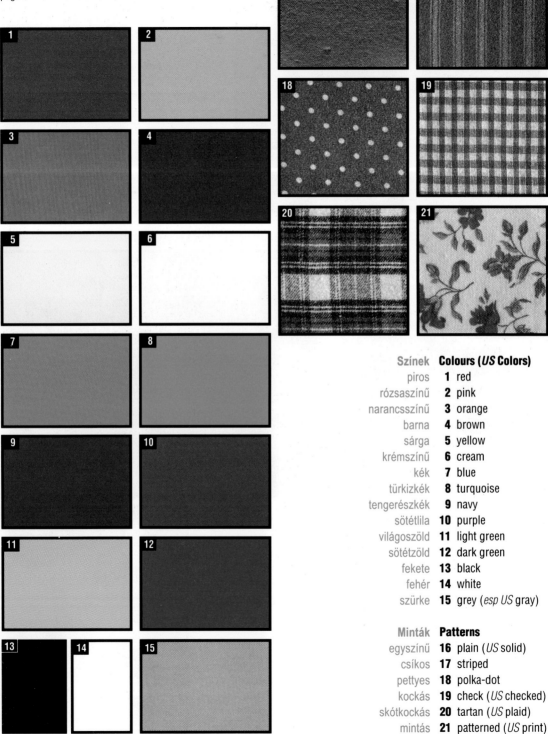

Színek		Colours (*US* Colors)
piros	**1**	red
rózsaszínű	**2**	pink
narancsszínű	**3**	orange
barna	**4**	brown
sárga	**5**	yellow
krémszínű	**6**	cream
kék	**7**	blue
türkizkék	**8**	turquoise
tengerészkék	**9**	navy
sötétlila	**10**	purple
világoszöld	**11**	light green
sötétzöld	**12**	dark green
fekete	**13**	black
fehér	**14**	white
szürke	**15**	grey (*esp US* gray)

Minták		Patterns
egyszínű	**16**	plain (*US* solid)
csíkos	**17**	striped
pettyes	**18**	polka-dot
kockás	**19**	check (*US* checked)
skótkockás	**20**	tartan (*US* plaid)
mintás	**21**	patterned (*US* print)

page 10

Clothes 1

2 /ay out
1
2
3
4
5
6
7
8
9
10
11
12
13
14
15
16
17
18
19
20
21
22
23

iskolai egyenruha	**1**	school uniform
sapka	**2**	cap
blézer	**3**	blazer
nadrág	**4**	trousers (*US* pants)
póló(trikó)	**5**	T-shirt
pulóver	**6**	sweater
farmernadrág	**7**	jeans
félkabát/zakó	**8**	jacket
blúz	**9**	blouse
kézitáska	**10**	handbag (*US also* purse)
szoknya	**11**	skirt
aktatáska	**12**	briefcase
csizma	**13**	boot
sál	**14**	scarf
kesztyű	**15**	glove
esernyő	**16**	umbrella
kabát	**17**	coat
öltöny	**18**	suit
ing	**19**	shirt
nyakkendő	**20**	tie
zsebkendő	**21**	handkerchief
ballonkabát/esőkabát	**22**	raincoat
cipő	**23**	shoe

Clothes 2 page 11

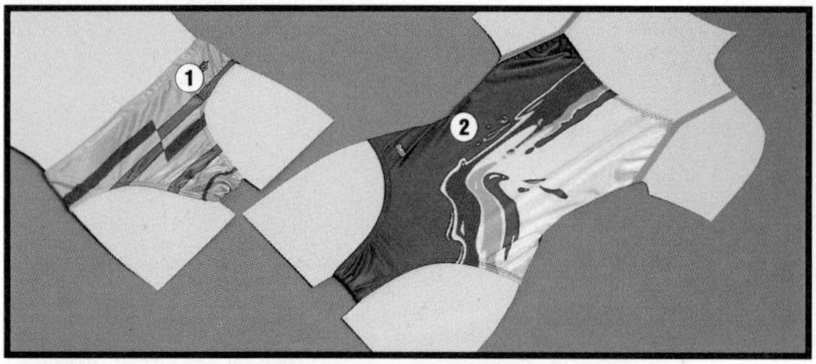
1
2

15
18
16
17

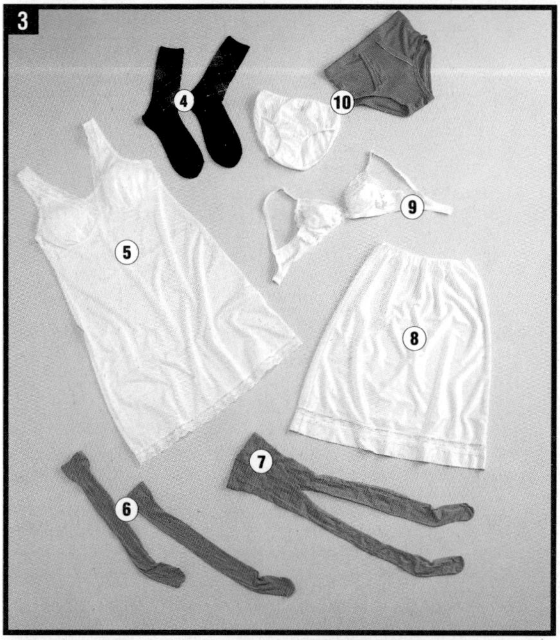
3
4
10
5
9
8
7
6

23
19
20
21
22

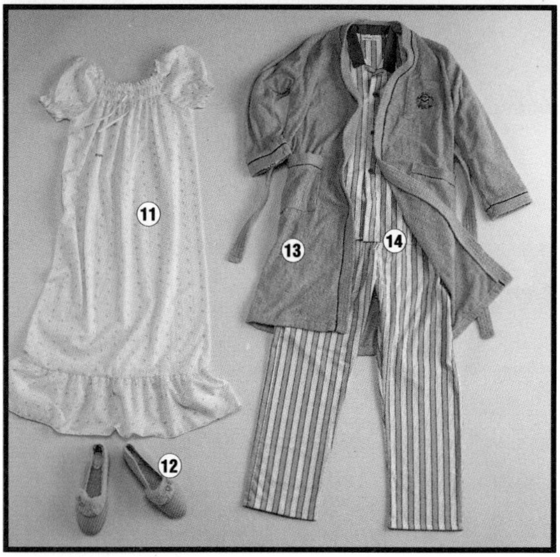
11
13
14
12

fürdőnadrág **1** swimming-trunks (*US* bathing suit)
fürdőruha **2** swimsuit (*US* bathing suit)
fehérnemű **3** underwear
zokni **4** socks
kombiné **5** full slip
harisnya **6** stockings
harisnyanadrág **7** tights (*US* pantyhose)
alsószoknya **8** half slip
melltartó **9** bra
alsónadrág **10** pants (*US* underpants)
hálóing **11** night-dress (*US* nightgown)
papucs **12** slipper
hálóköntös **13** dressing gown (*US* robe)
pizsama **14** pyjamas (*US* pajamas)
gallér **15** collar
ujj **16** sleeve
mandzsetta **17** cuff
zseb **18** pocket
csat **19** buckle
sarok **20** heel
tárca **21** wallet
pénztárca **22** purse (*US* wallet)
cipőfűző **23** shoelace

Dressing up

1
5
9
13
16
17
2
6
18
LAZER
10
14
7
19
11
3
15
12
4
8
21
20

autóversenyző	**1** racing driver (*US* race car driver)
bukósisak	**2** helmet
tréningruha	**3** track suit (*US also* jogging suit)
edzőcipő	**4** trainer (*US* sneaker)
cigány	**5** gypsy
sál	**6** scarf
kardigán	**7** cardigan
szandál	**8** sandal
bokszoló	**9** boxer
trikó	**10** vest (*US* tank top)
öv	**11** belt
rövidnadrág	**12** shorts
szörnyeteg	**13** monster
melegítőfelső	**14** sweatshirt
karóra	**15** watch
boszorkány	**16** witch
kalap	**17** hat
napszemüveg	**18** sun-glasses
(női)ruha	**19** dress
smink	**20** make-up
rúzs	**21** lipstick

27
22
26
25
23
24

Ékszerek	**Jewellery (*esp US* Jewelry)**
bross/kitűző	**22** brooch (*US* pin)
karkötő	**23** bracelet
gyűrű	**24** ring
lánc	**25** chain
nyaklánc	**26** necklace
fülbevaló	**27** earring

Buildings 1 page 13

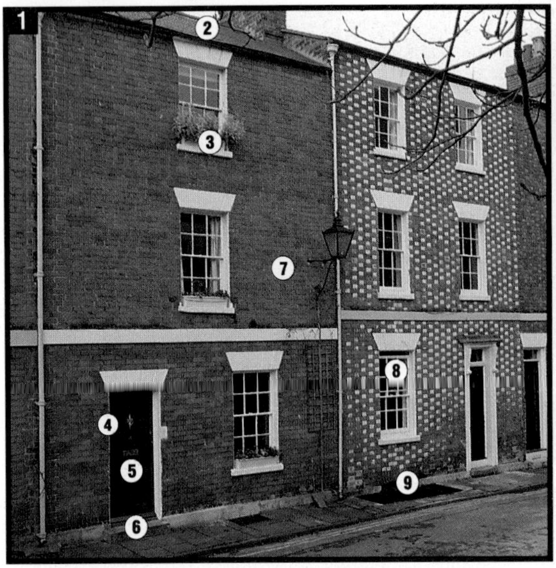
1
2
3
4
5
6
7
8
9

10
11
12
13
14
15

sorház **1** terraced house (*US* town house)
palatető **2** slate roof
virágláda **3** window-box
kopogtató **4** knocker
levélszekrény **5** letter-box (*US* mailbox)
küszöb **6** doorstep
téglafal **7** brick wall
tolóablak **8** sash window
pinceablak **9** basement window
tömbház **10** block of flats (*US* apartment house)
legfelső emelet **11** top floor
erkély **12** balcony
első emelet **13** first floor (*US* second floor)
földszint **14** ground floor (*US also* first floor)
parkoló **15** car-park (*US* parking lot)

Építőanyagok **Building Materials**

tégla **16** brick
kő **17** stone
beton **18** concrete
tetőcserép **19** tile
pala **20** slate
nád **21** thatch
fa **22** wood
üveg **23** glass

16

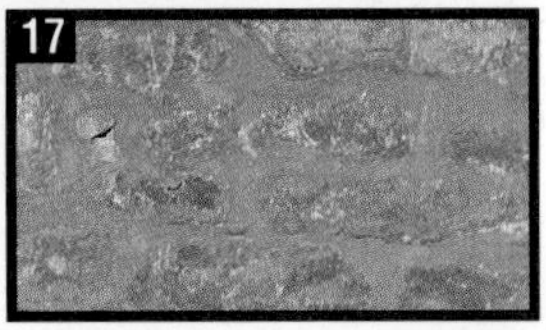
17

18

19

20

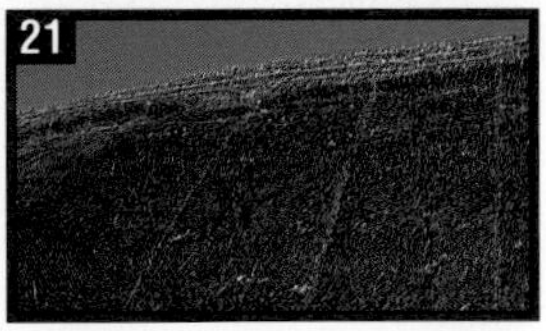
21

22

23

page 14

Buildings 2

1
2
3
4
5

13
14
15
16
17
18

6
7
8
9
10
11
12

19
20
21
22
23

családi ház **1** detached house (*US* one-family house)
garázs **2** garage
bejárati ajtó **3** front door
oszlop **4** pillar
spaletta **5** shutter
ikerház **6** semi-detached house (*US* two-family house)
kémény **7** chimney
ablak **8** window
ablakpárkány **9** window-sill/window-ledge
ív **10** arch
kiugró ablakfülke **11** bay window
betonkerítés **12** concrete wall

villa/vidéki ház **13** cottage
nádtető **14** thatched roof
manzárdablak **15** dormer
tornác **16** porch
(fa)kapu **17** wooden gate
kőkerítés **18** stone wall
földszintes családi ház **19** bungalow (*US* ranch house)
TV-antenna **20** TV aerial (*US* antenna)
esőcsatorna **21** drainpipe
ereszcsatorna **22** gutter
cseréptető **23** tiled roof

The Dining-room page15

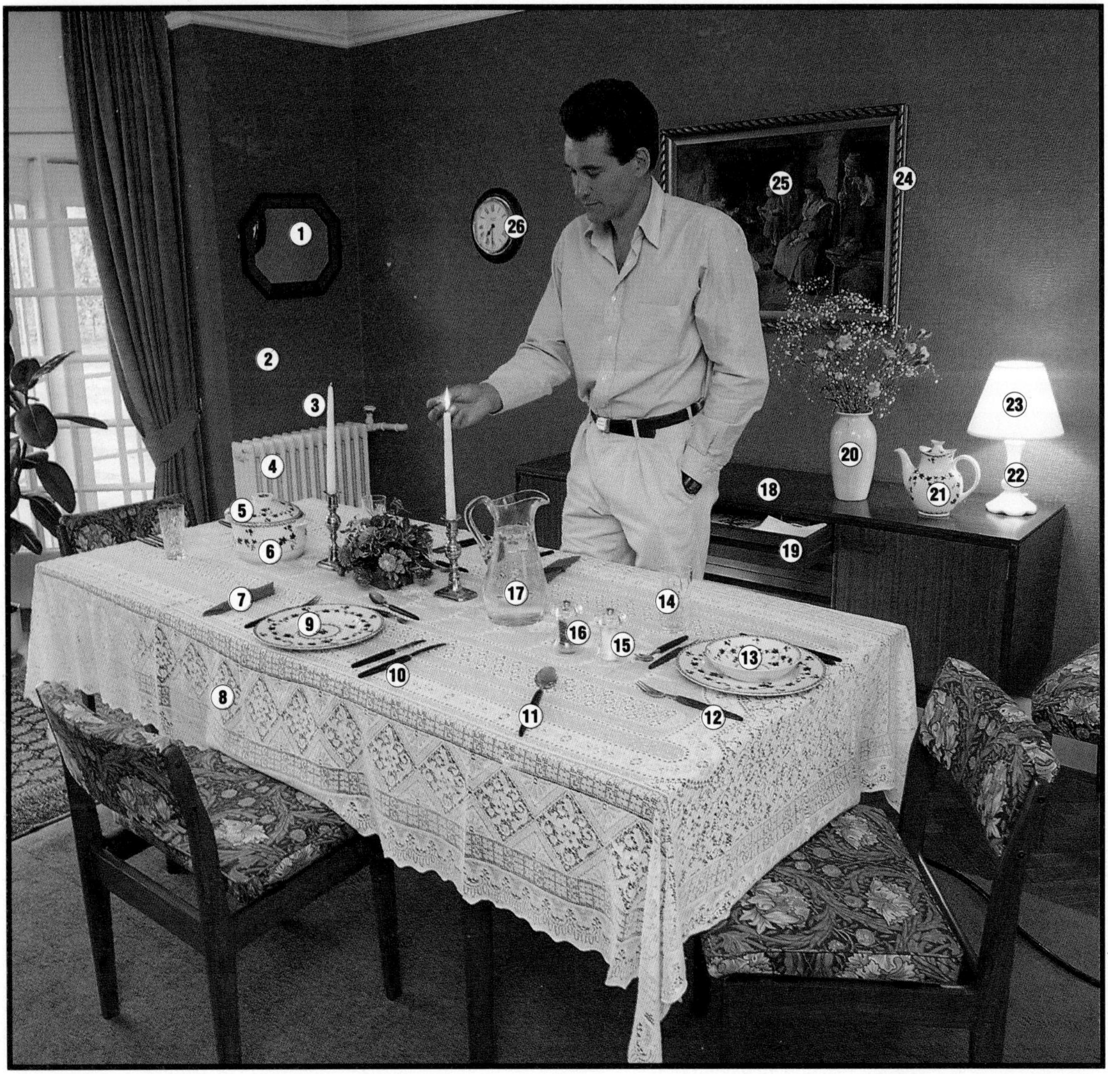

1
2
3
4
5
6
7
8
9
10
11
12
13
14
15
16
17
18
19
20
21
22
23
24
25
26

tükör	**1** mirror	pohár	**14** glass
fal	**2** wall	só	**15** salt
gyertya	**3** candle	bors	**16** pepper
radiátor	**4** radiator	kancsó	**17** jug (*US* pitcher)
fedő	**5** lid	tálalószekrény	**18** sideboard (*US* buffet)
(tálaló)edény	**6** dish	fiók	**19** drawer
szalvéta	**7** napkin	váza	**20** vase
asztalterítő	**8** table-cloth	kávéskancsó	**21** coffee-pot
lapostányér	**9** plate	lámpa	**22** lamp
kés	**10** knife	lámpaernyő	**23** lampshade
(evő)kanál	**11** spoon	keret	**24** frame
villa	**12** fork	festmény	**25** painting
mélytányér	**13** bowl	(fali)óra	**26** clock

The Living-room

1
2
3
4
5
6
7
8
9
10
11
12
13
14
15
16
17
18
19
20
21
22
23
24

mennyezet	**1** ceiling	csészealj	**13** saucer
kandallópárkány	**2** mantelpiece (*US* mantel)	csésze	**14** cup
kandalló	**3** fireplace	kávéskanál	**15** teaspoon
tűz	**4** fire	papírkosár	**16** waste-paper basket
fahasáb	**5** log	kanapé	**17** sofa (*esp US* couch)
szőnyeg	**6** rug	párna	**18** cushion
szőnyegpadló	**7** carpet	növény	**19** plant
dohányzóasztal	**8** coffee-table	függönyök	**20** curtains (*US* drapes)
távirányító	**9** remote control	elemes bútor	**21** wall unit
süteménydoboz	**10** biscuit tin (*US* cookie tin)	fotel	**22** armchair
teáskancsó	**11** teapot	televízió/TV	**23** television/TV
tálca	**12** tray	(kazettás) videomagnó	**24** video cassette recorder/VCR

The Bathroom page 17

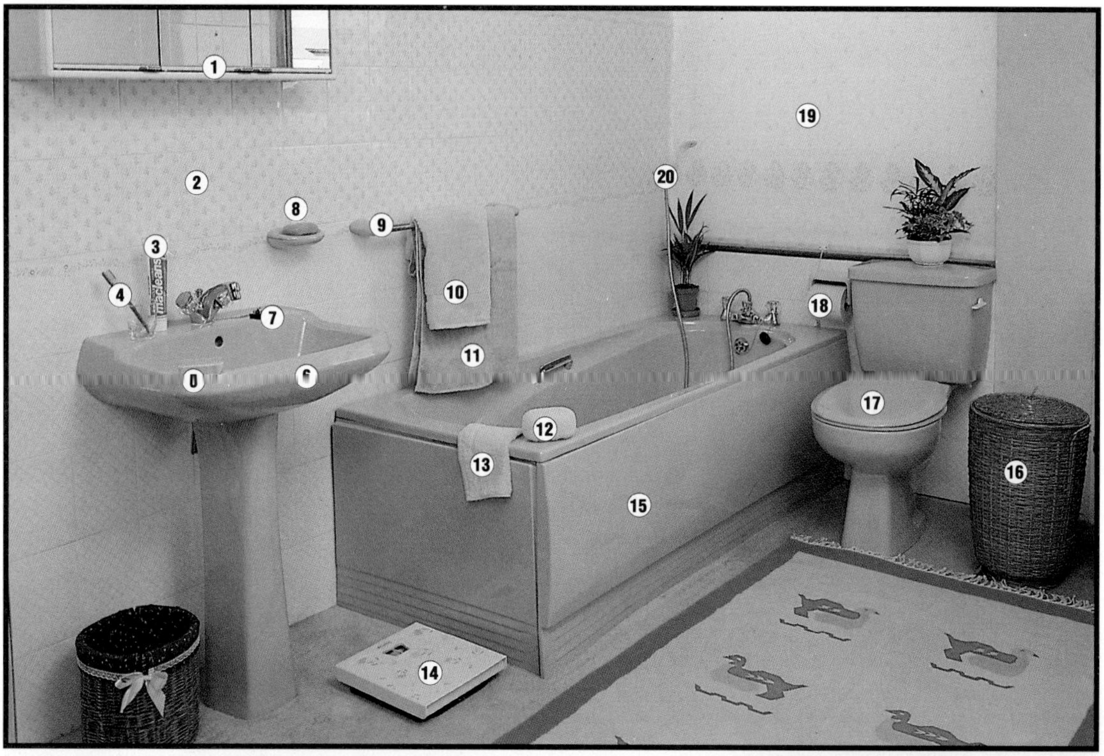
1
2
3
4
5
6
7
8
9
10
11
12
13
14
15
16
17
18
19
20

fürdőszoba-szekrény	**1**	bathroom cabinet (*US* medicine chest/cabinet)
csempe	**2**	tile
(egy) tubus fogkrém	**3**	tube of toothpaste
fogkefe	**4**	toothbrush
körömkefe	**5**	nail-brush
mosdókagyló	**6**	wash-basin (*US* sink)
dugó	**7**	plug (*US* stopper)
(egy) darab szappan	**8**	bar of soap
törölközőtartó	**9**	towel-rail (*US* towel rack)
kéztörlő	**10**	hand-towel
fürdőlepedő	**11**	bath-towel
szivacs	**12**	sponge
mosdókesztyű	**13**	flannel (*US* washcloth)
(fürdőszoba-)mérleg	**14**	(bathroom) scales (*US* scale)
fürdőkád	**15**	bath (*US* bathtub)
szennyeskosár	**16**	laundry basket (*US* hamper)
vécé/toalett	**17**	toilet
vécépapír	**18**	toilet paper
ablakroló	**19**	blind (*US* shade)
zuhany	**20**	shower

21
22
23
24
25
26
27
28

borotválkozás utáni arcszesz	**21**	aftershave (*US* after-shave lotion)
villanyborotva	**22**	electric razor
borotva	**23**	razor
borotvapenge	**24**	razor-blade
borotvahab	**25**	shaving-foam (*US* shaving cream)
sampon	**26**	shampoo
fésű	**27**	comb
hintőpor	**28**	talcum powder (*also* talc)

The Bedroom

chagall
Royal Academy of Arts
11 January to 31 March

fésülködőasztal	**1** dressing table (*US* dresser)
ágynemű	**2** bed-linen
ágy	**3** bed
ágyterítő	**4** bedspread
takaró	**5** blanket
lepedő	**6** sheet
párnahuzat	**7** pillowcase
hajkefe	**8** hairbrush
(egy) doboz papírzsebkendő	**9** box of tissues
éjjeliszekrény	**10** bedside cabinet (*US* night table)
matrac	**11** mattress
párna	**12** pillow
ágyvég	**13** headboard
ébresztőóra	**14** alarm clock
plakát	**15** poster
lámpa	**16** light
ruhásszekrény	**17** wardrobe (*US* closet)
ruhaakasztó	**18** coat-hanger (*esp US* hanger)
komód	**19** chest of drawers (*US also* bureau)
hajszárító	**20** hair-drier (*or* hair-dryer)

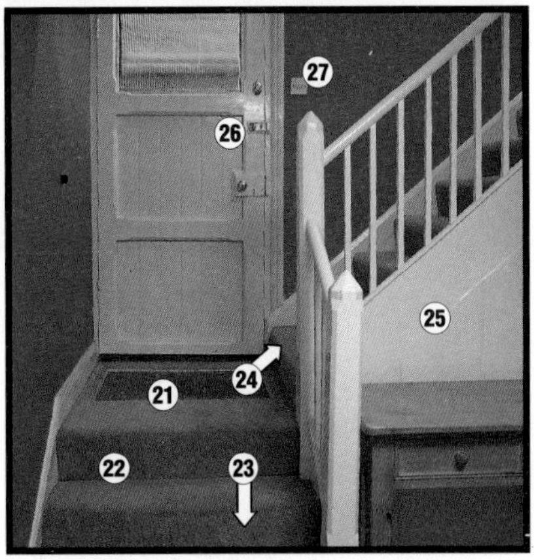

lábtörlő	**21** doormat
lépcső(fok)	**22** stair (*esp US* step)
lent/(a) földszinten	**23** downstairs
fent/(az) emeleten	**24** upstairs
lépcső	**25** staircase
zár	**26** lock
villanykapcsoló	**27** light switch

The Utility Room (*US also* Laundry Room)

dreft
Dulux
RONSEAL
Chrome Polish

mosószer	**1**	detergent
mosogató	**2**	sink
mosógép	**3**	washing-machine
szemétlapát	**4**	dustpan
kefe	**5**	brush
vödör	**6**	bucket (*esp US* pail)
porszívó	**7**	vacuum cleaner (*Brit also* Hoover)
felmosó	**8**	mop
vasalódeszka	**9**	ironing-board
ruhacsipesz	**10**	clothes-peg (*US* clothespin)
(vasaló)zsinór	**11**	flex (*esp US* cord)
csatlakozódugó	**12**	plug
vasaló	**13**	iron
portörlő ruha	**14**	duster (*US* dust cloth)
villanyégő	**15**	light-bulb
akasztókampó	**16**	hook
elemlámpa	**17**	torch (*US* flashlight)
súrolókefe	**18**	scrubbing-brush (*US* scrub brush)
hideg(víz)-csap	**19**	cold(-water) tap (*US* cold water faucet)
meleg(víz)-csap	**20**	hot(-water) tap (*US* hot water faucet)
konnektor	**21**	socket (*US also* outlet)
ruhaszárító-kötél	**22**	clothes-line

The Kitchen

1
2
3
4
5
6
7
8
9
10
11
12
13
14
15
16
17
18
19
20
21
22
23
24
25
26
27

tűzálló tál	**1**	casserole
szita	**2**	sieve (*esp US* strainer)
keverőtál	**3**	mixing bowl
szakácskönyv	**4**	cookery book (*US* cookbook)
mosogatószer	**5**	washing-up liquid (*US* dishwashing liquid)
dörzsszivacs	**6**	scourer (*US* scouring pad)
konyharuha	**7**	tea towel (*US* dish towel)
habverőgép	**8**	mixer
szűrő(edény)	**9**	colander
konzervnyitó	**10**	tin-opener (*US* can opener)
merőkanál	**11**	ladle
sodrófa	**12**	rolling-pin
munkafelület	**13**	work surface (*US* counter)
hűtőszekrény	**14**	fridge (*esp US* refrigerator)
mélyhűtő	**15**	freezer
bögre	**16**	mug
kenyérpirító	**17**	toaster
kenyérvágó-deszka	**18**	breadboard (*US* cutting board)
elektromos vízforraló	**19**	kettle (*US* electric teakettle)
(konyha)szekrény	**20**	cupboard (*esp US* cabinet)
fogókesztyű	**21**	oven glove (*US* pot holder)
sütő	**22**	oven
polc	**23**	shelf
palacsintasütő/serpenyő	**24**	frying-pan
háztartási robotgép	**25**	food processor
nyeles lábas	**26**	saucepan/pot
gázrózsa	**27**	burner

Tools page 21

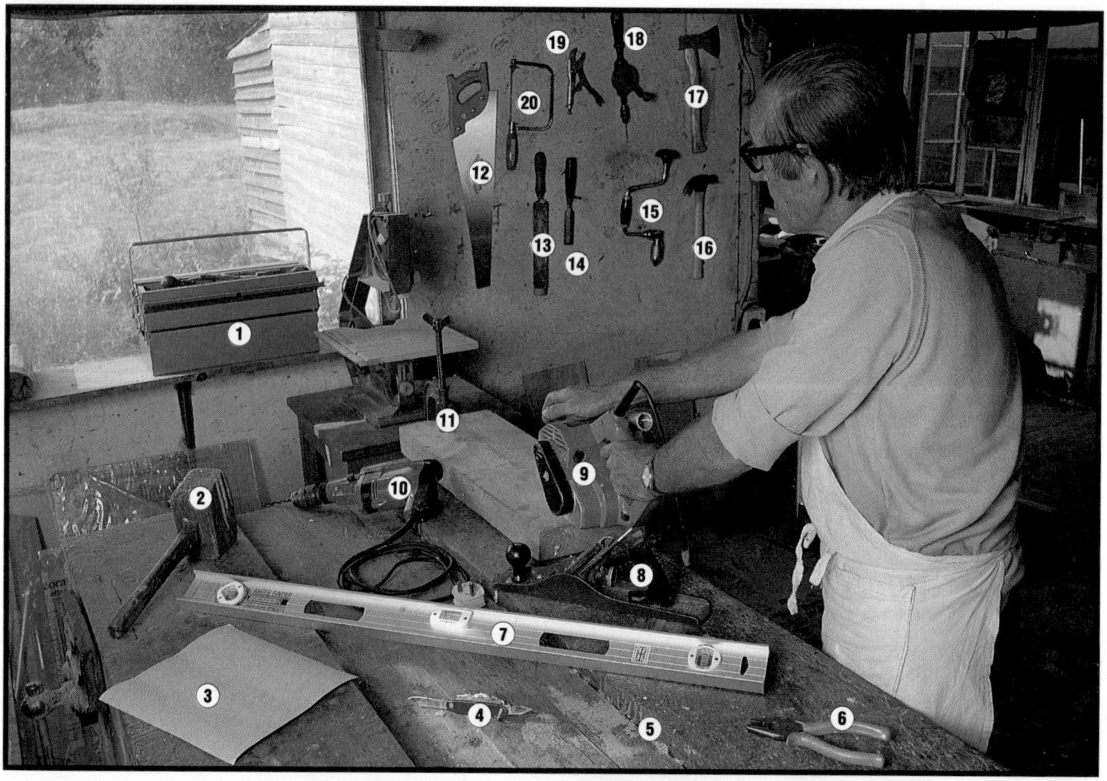
1
2
3
4
5
6
7
8
9
10
11
12
13
14
15
16
17
18
19
20

szerszámosláda	**1** tool-box
fakalapács	**2** mallet
dörzspapír	**3** sandpaper
zsebkés	**4** penknife (*esp US* pocketknife)
munkapad/gyalupad	**5** workbench
(kombinált)fogó	**6** pliers
vízmérték	**7** spirit-level (*US* level)
gyalu	**8** plane
villanyfűrész	**9** power saw
villanyfúró	**10** electric drill
satu	**11** vice (*US* vise)
kézifűrész	**12** handsaw (*esp US* saw)
reszelő	**13** file
véső	**14** chisel
amerikáner	**15** brace
kalapács	**16** hammer
kisbalta	**17** hatchet
kézifúró	**18** hand drill
csőrösfogó	**19** wrench
lombfűrész	**20** coping saw

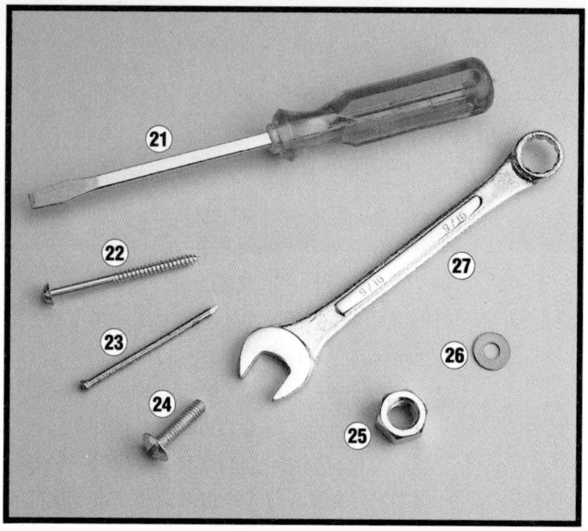
21
22
23
24
25
26
27

csavarhúzó	**21** screwdriver
csavar	**22** screw
szög	**23** nail
vascsavar	**24** bolt
anyacsavar	**25** nut
csavaralátét	**26** washer
csavarkulcs	**27** spanner (*US* wrench)

page 22

The Garden

1
2
15
14
17
19
18
20
16
13
12
3
8
5
9
7
4
11
10
6

hátsó kert **1** back garden (*US* backyard)
hinta **2** swing
fű/gyep **3** grass/lawn
fa **4** tree
fűnyírógép **5** lawnmower
öntözőkanna **6** watering-can
gereblye **7** rake
nyesőolló **8** shears
bokor **9** bush
virágcserép **10** flowerpot
terasz **11** patio
kertészlapát **12** trowel
seprű **13** broom
kerti pad **14** bench
kerítés **15** fence
nyárson sütés **16** barbecue
talicska **17** wheelbarrow
villa **18** fork
ásó **19** spade
szemétvödör **20** dustbin (*US* garbage can)

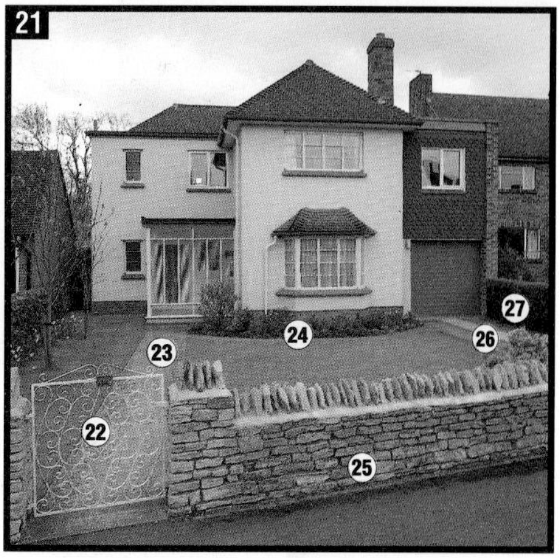
21
27
24
26
23
22
25

előkert **21** front garden (*US* front yard)
kapu **22** gate
járda **23** path (*US* front walk)
virágágy **24** flower-bed
fal **25** wall
kocsibejáró **26** drive (*US* driveway)
sövény **27** hedge

In the Market 1 page 23

1
2
3
4
5
6
7
8
9
10
11
12
13
14
15
16
17
18
19
20
21
22

Zöldségek		**Vegetables**
stand	**1**	market stall (*US* stand)
fokhagyma	**2**	garlic
zöldpaprika	**3**	green pepper
karfiol	**4**	cauliflower
spárga	**5**	asparagus
retek	**6**	radish
fejes saláta	**7**	lettuce
cékla	**8**	beetroot (*US* beet)
burgonya	**9**	potato
uborka	**10**	cucumber
vöröshagyma	**11**	onion
cukkini	**12**	courgette (*US* zucchini)
zsázsa	**13**	watercress
sárgarépa	**14**	carrot
kelbimbó	**15**	Brussels sprout (*US* brussels sprout)
zeller	**16**	celery
brokkoli	**17**	broccoli
fehérrépa	**18**	turnip
paradicsom	**19**	tomato
padlizsán	**20**	aubergine (*US* eggplant)
káposzta	**21**	cabbage
papírzacskó	**22**	paper bag

page 24

In the Market 2

1
2
3
4
5
6
7
8
9
10
11
12
13
14
15
16
17
18
19
20
21
22

Gyümölcsök	**Fruit**
sárgadinnye	**1** melon
(egy) doboz földieper	**2** punnet of strawberries (*US* basket of strawberries)
(egy) fürt banán	**3** bunch of bananas
alma	**4** apple
földimogyoró	**5** peanut
citrom	**6** lemon
kókuszdió	**7** coconut
ananász	**8** pineapple
narancs	**9** orange
(egy) fürt szőlő	**10** bunch of grapes
őszibarack	**11** peach
(egy) zacskó dió	**12** bag of nuts
avokádó	**13** avocado
papaya	**14** pawpaw (*esp US* papaya)
licsi	**15** lychee (*also* litchi)
körte	**16** pear
lime	**17** lime
kiwi	**18** kiwi fruit
mangó	**19** mango
szilva	**20** plum
grépfrút	**21** grapefruit
kosár-oszlop	**22** stack of baskets

At the Florist's page 25

fenyőfa/karácsonyfa	**1** pine tree (*also* Christmas tree)	krizantém	**15** chrysanthemum
törzs	**2** trunk	pálma	**16** palm
gyökerek	**3** roots	rózsa	**17** rose
virágszirom	**4** petal	orchidea	**18** orchid
páfrány	**5** fern	szár	**19** stem
kosár	**6** basket	frézia	**20** freesia
ág	**7** branch	kaktusz	**21** cactus
fakéreg	**8** bark	fenyőtoboz	**22** pine cone
(egy) csokor szárazvirág	**9** bunch of dried flowers	margaréta	**23** daisy
szárazvirág-kompozíció	**10** dried flower arrangement	szegfű	**24** carnation
levél	**11** leaf	tulipán	**25** tulip
bonsai	**12** bonsai	liliom	**26** lily
virághagyma	**13** bulb	bimbó	**27** bud
nárcisz	**14** daffodil	írisz	**28** iris

At the Newsagent's (*US* Newsstand)

Írószer	**Stationery**
(egy) tekercs cellux	**1** reel of Sellotape (*US* roll of Scotch tape)
(egy) gombolyag madzag	**2** ball of string
(egy) köteg boríték	**3** packet of envelopes (*US* pack of envelopes)
levélpapír	**4** writing-paper
színes filctoll-készlet	**5** set of coloured pens (*US* set of colored pens)
(egy) tekercs csomagolópapír	**6** roll of wrapping paper
(egy) sor képes folyóirat	**7** row of magazines
(egy) köteg újság	**8** pile of newspapers

Édességek	**Confectionery (*US* Candy)**
(egy) doboz csokoládé	**9** box of chocolates (*US* box of chocolate)
(egy) zacskó cukorka	**10** bag of sweets (*US* bag of candy)
(egy) tábla csokoládé	**11** bar of chocolate
dupla csomag	**12** twin-pack
tripla csomag	**13** triple-pack
(egy) csomag cukorka	**14** packet of sweets (*US* pack of candy)
(egy) rollni cukorka	**15** packet of sweets (*US* roll of candy)
(egy) csomag burgonyaszirom	**16** packet of crisps (*US* bag of potato chips)
csokoládé	**17** chocolate
édesség/cukorka	**18** sweets (*US* candy)
burgonyaszirom	**19** crisps (*US* potato chips)

At the Delicatessen page 27

CORN FLAKES
1
2
3
4
5
6
7
8
9
10
11
12
13
14

19
20
21
22
23
24
25
26

(egy) doboz kukoricapehely	**1**	box of cereal
egész kenyér	**2**	loaf of bread
szendvicsek	**3**	sandwiches
zsemle	**4**	roll
(egy) üveg dzsem/lekvár	**5**	jar of jam/pot of jam
tonhalkonzerv	**6**	tin of tuna (*US* can of tuna)
sült hús	**7**	joint of cooked meat (*US* roast)
(egy) szelet hús	**8**	slice of meat
sült csirke	**9**	roast chicken
(egy) darab csirke	**10**	chicken portion (*US* piece of chicken)
húsos lepény	**11**	pie
(egy) darab húsos lepény	**12**	piece of pie
(egy) tucat tojás	**13**	dozen eggs
fél tucat tojás	**14**	half a dozen eggs
keksz	**15**	biscuit (*US* cookie)
(egy) csomag keksz	**16**	packet of biscuits (*US* package of cookies)
dzsem/lekvár	**17**	jam
tonhal	**18**	tuna

(egy) pohár joghurt	**19**	pot of yoghurt (*US* container of yogurt)
(egy) doboz margarin	**20**	tub of margarine
(egy) doboz narancslé	**21**	carton of orange juice
sajt	**22**	cheese
töltött olajbogyó	**23**	stuffed olives
fél liter tej	**24**	pint of milk
(egy) üveg ásványvíz	**25**	bottle of mineral water
(egy) doboz szénsavas üdítőital	**26**	can of fizzy drink (*US* can of soda)
joghurt	**27**	yoghurt (*esp US* yogurt)
margarin	**28**	margarine
vaj	**29**	butter

27
28
29

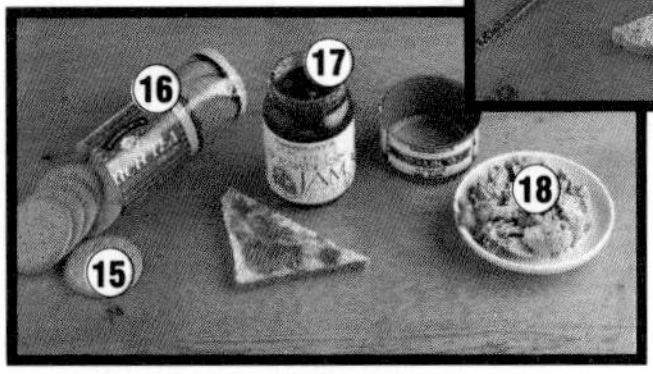
15
16
17
18

At the Restaurant

page 28

1
2
3
4
5

6
7
8
9
10
11
12
13

14
15
16
17
18
19
20
21
22
23
24
25
26
27

Előételek	**Starters (*US* Appetizers)**
cseresznye	**1** cherry
sárgadinnye	**2** melon
füstölt lazac	**3** smoked salmon
pástétom pirítóssal	**4** pâté with toast
paradicsomleves	**5** tomato soup
Desszertek	**Desserts**
zsúrkocsi	**6** dessert trolley (*US* dessert cart)
gyümölcs	**7** fruit
almáspite	**8** apple pie
sajttorta	**9** cheesecake
málnafagylalt	**10** raspberry ice-cream
gyümölcskoktél	**11** fruit cocktail
tejszín(hab)	**12** cream
csokoládétorta	**13** chocolate gateau (*US* chocolate cake)

pincér	**14** waiter
étlap	**15** menu
Főételek	**Main Courses**
marhasült	**16** roast beef
pisztráng mandulával	**17** trout with almonds
bifsztek	**18** steak
(sült) bárányszeletek	**19** lamb chops
(**Zöldség**)**köretek**	**Vegetables**
csemegekukorica	**20** sweet corn (*US* corn)
gomba	**21** mushrooms
saláta	**22** salad
zöldbab	**23** runner beans (*US* string beans)
zöldborsó	**24** peas
héjában sült burgonya	**25** jacket potato (*esp US* baked potato)
főtt burgonya	**26** boiled potatoes
sült hasábburgonya	**27** chips (*US* French fries)

At the Camera Shop (*US* Camera Store)

SALE
SALE
1
2
3
4
5
6
7
8
Camera

15
16
17
18
Nikon

19
20
21
22

9
10
11

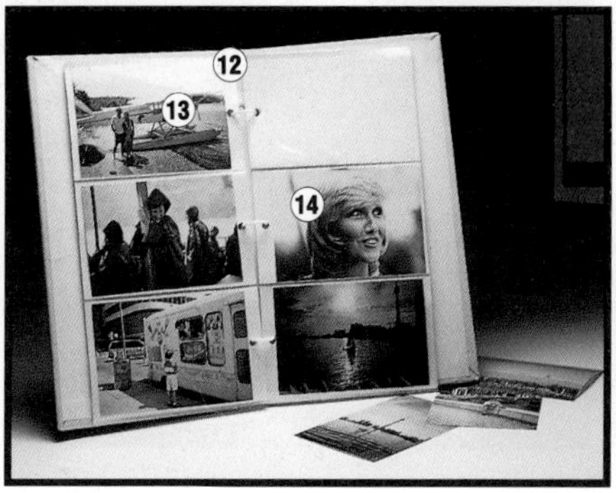
12
13
14

23
Polaroid
Supercolor

vevő	**1**	customer
blokk/számla	**2**	receipt
pénztárgép	**3**	cash register
fotóállvány	**4**	tripod
távcső/teleszkóp	**5**	telescope
eladó	**6**	shop assistant (*US* salesperson)
látcső	**7**	binoculars
diavetítő	**8**	slide projector
dia(kép)	**9**	slide
negatív	**10**	negative
(egy) tekercs film	**11**	reel of film (*US* roll of film)
fotóalbum	**12**	photo album
színes fénykép	**13**	colour print (*US* color print)
fekete-fehér fénykép	**14**	black and white print

zoom/gumiobjektív	**15**	zoom lens
tükörreflexes fényképezőgép	**16**	single lens reflex/SLR camera
lencse/objektív	**17**	lens
villanófény/vaku	**18**	flash (gun)
35 mm-es automata fényképezőgép	**19**	35 mm* compact camera
beépített vaku	**20**	built-in flash
fényképezőgép-tok	**21**	camera case
tartószíj	**22**	strap
polaroid fényképezőgép	**23**	polaroid camera

milliméter **mm = millimetre (US millimeter)*

At the Hi-fi Shop (*US* Electronics Store)

3
2
Panasonic
1
4

5
7
6
SONY

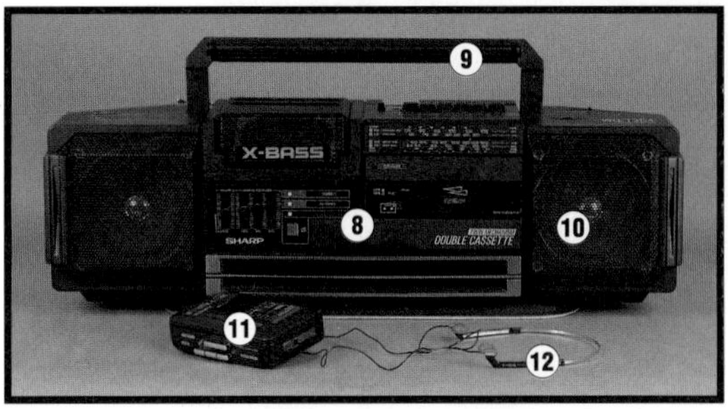
9
X-BASS
SHARP
8
DOUBLE CASSETTE
10
11
12

13
14
PIONEER
15
PIONEER
16
HIGH POWER OUTPUT
PIONEER
17
PIONEER
18
SONY
19
COMPACT DISC PLAYER

camcorder **1** camcorder
mikrofon **2** microphone
kereső **3** viewfinder
videokazetta **4** (video)tape
hanglemez **5** record
(magnó)kazetta **6** cassette
kompaktlemez **7** compact disc/CD
(kazettás) magnósrádió **8** radio cassette recorder (*US also* AM/FM cassette recorder)
fogantyú **9** handle
hangszóró **10** speaker
Walkman **11** Walkman (*Brit also* personal stereo)
fejhallgató **12** headphones

hi-fi-torony **13** stereo/stereo system (*US also* sound system) (*Brit also* hi-fi)
lemezjátszó-korong **14** turntable
rádió **15** radio
erősítő **16** amplifier
hangszín-szabályozó **17** graphic equalizer
magnó **18** cassette deck/tape deck
kompakt-lemezjátszó **19** compact disc player/ CD player

Postal Services 1

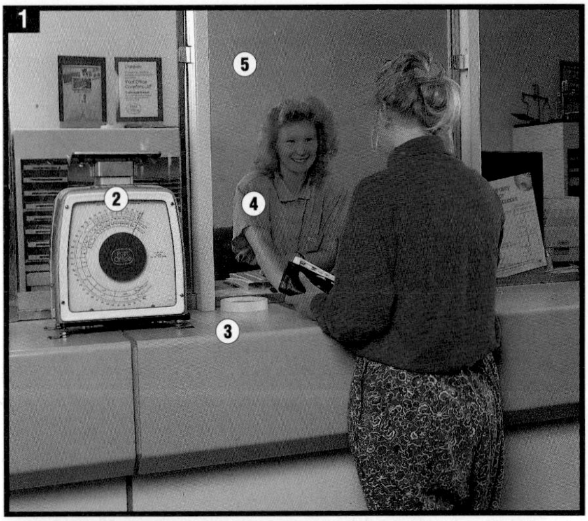
1
2
3
4
5

15
16

17
Royal Mail stamps

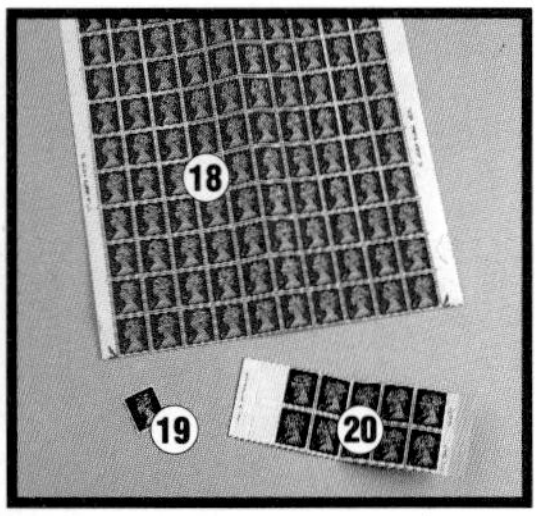
18
19
20

6
7
8
9
10
11
Royal Mail
Please use the Postcode

12
13
14

postahivatal	**1**	post office
mérleg	**2**	scales (*US* scale)
pult	**3**	counter
postai alkalmazott	**4**	counter assistant (*US* postal clerk)
ablak	**5**	window
postaláda-ürítés	**6**	collection
postaautó	**7**	post office van (*US* mail truck)
postás/kézbesítő	**8**	postman (*US* mailman)
postazsák	**9**	mailbag
postai küldemény	**10**	post (*US* mail)
postaláda	**11**	letter-box/postbox (*US* mailbox)
kézbesítés	**12**	delivery
postástáska	**13**	postbag (*esp US* mailbag)
levélszekrény	**14**	letter-box (*US* mailbox)
expresszküldemény-kézbesítés	**15**	delivery by courier (*US* delivery by messenger)
expresszküldemény-kézbesítő	**16**	despatch-rider (*US* messenger)
bélyegautomata	**17**	stamp machine
(egy) levél bélyeg	**18**	sheet of stamps
bélyeg	**19**	stamp
bélyegkönyvecske	**20**	book of stamps

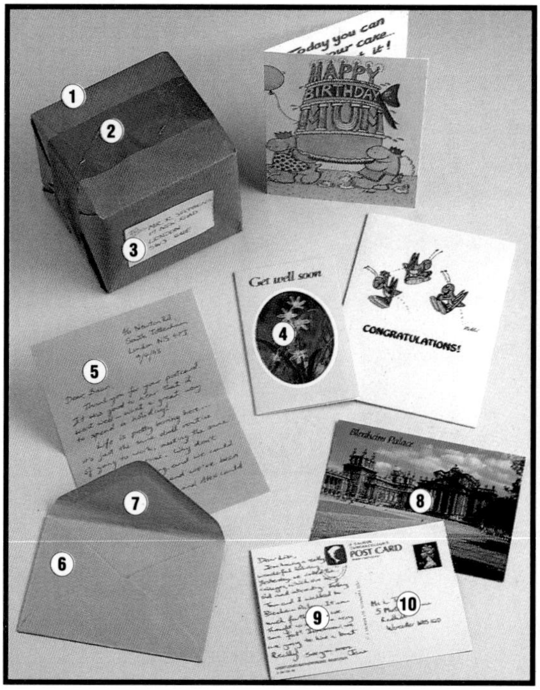

HAPPY BIRTHDAY MUM
Get well soon
CONGRATULATIONS!
POST CARD
1
2
3
4
5
6
7
8
9
10

page 32 **Postal Services 2**

Brit angol ***British*** Amerikai angol ***American***

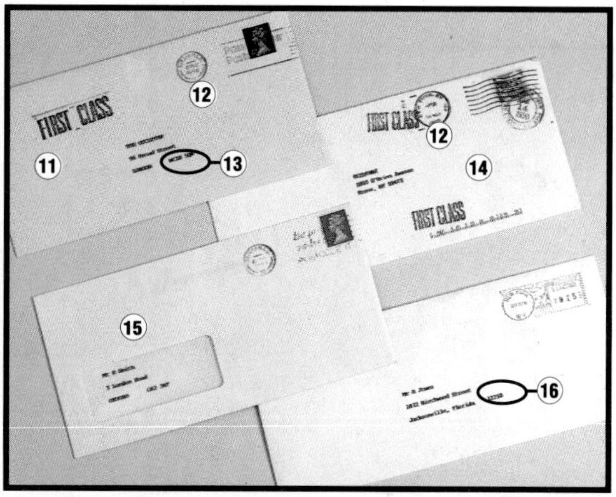

FIRST CLASS
11
12
13
14
15
16

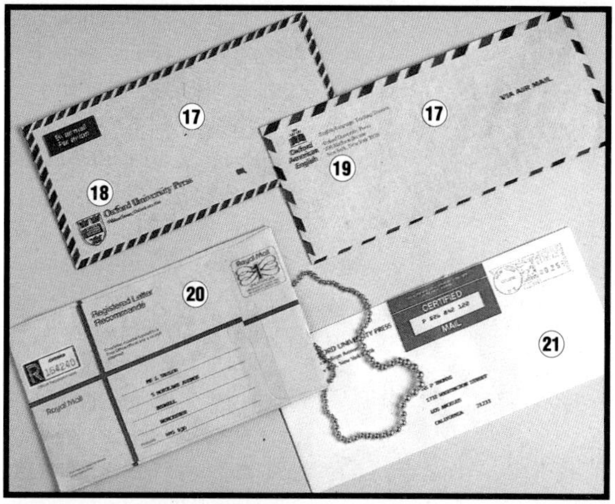

VIA AIR MAIL
CERTIFIED MAIL
Royal Mail
17
18
19
20
21

BRITISH POSTAL ORDER
FIVE POUNDS
CHASE
Money Order
22
23

Royal Mail
24

EXPRESS MAIL SERVICE
25

csomag	**1** parcel (*esp US* package)
ragasztószalag	**2** tape
címke	**3** label
üdvözlő lap	**4** greetings card (*US* greeting card)
levél	**5** letter
boríték	**6** envelope
ragasztós hátrész	**7** flap
képeslap	**8** postcard
üzenet	**9** message
cím	**10** address
expresszlevél	**11** first-class post (*Brit*)
postabélyegző	**12** postmark
irányítószám	**13** postcode (*also* postal code) (*Brit*)
expresszlevél	**14** first class mail (*US*)
(sima) levél	**15** second-class post (*Brit*)
irányítószám	**16** zip code (*US*)
légiposta	**17** airmail
(a) feladó (címe)	**18** address of sender (*Brit*)
(a) feladó (címe)	**19** return address (*US*)
ajánlott küldemény	**20** registered post (*Brit*)
ajánlott küldemény	**21** certified mail (*US*)
pénzesutalvány	**22** postal order (*Brit*)
pénzesutalvány	**23** money order (*US*)
expressz kézbesítés	**24** Special Delivery (*Brit*)
expressz kézbesítés	**25** Express Mail (*US*)

Numbers/The Date page 33

JULY 1998					
Sunday		5	12	19	26
Monday		6	13	20	27
Tuesday		7	14	21	28
Wednesday	1	8	15	22	29
Thursday	2	9	16	23	30
Friday	3	10	17	24	31
Saturday	4	11	18	25	

egy	**1**	one
kettő	**2**	two
három	**3**	three
négy	**4**	four
öt	**5**	five
hat	**6**	six
hét	**7**	seven
nyolc	**8**	eight
kilenc	**9**	nine
tíz	**10**	ten
tizenegy	**11**	eleven
tizenkettő	**12**	twelve
tizenhárom	**13**	thirteen
tizennégy	**14**	fourteen
tizenöt	**15**	fifteen
tizenhat	**16**	sixteen
tizenhét	**17**	seventeen
tizennyolc	**18**	eighteen
tizenkilenc	**19**	nineteen
húsz	**20**	twenty
huszonegy	**21**	twenty-one
harminc	**30**	thirty
negyven	**40**	forty
ötven	**50**	fifty
hatvan	**60**	sixty
hetven	**70**	seventy
nyolcvan	**80**	eighty
kilencven	**90**	ninety
(egy)száz	**100**	one hundred
százegy	**101**	one hundred and one
(egy)ezer	**1000**	one thousand
kétezer-kétszáztíz	**2210**	two thousand, two hundred and ten
egymillió	**1000000**	one million

1. első	**1st**	first
2. második	**2nd**	second
3. harmadik	**3rd**	third
4. negyedik	**4th**	fourth
5. ötödik	**5th**	fifth
6. hatodik	**6th**	sixth
7. hetedik	**7th**	seventh
8. nyolcadik	**8th**	eighth
9. kilencedik	**9th**	ninth
10. tizedik	**10th**	tenth
11. tizenegyedik	**11th**	eleventh
12. tizenkettedik	**12th**	twelfth
13. tizenharmadik	**13th**	thirteenth
20. huszadik	**20th**	twentieth
21. huszonegyedik	**21st**	twenty-first
22. huszonkettedik	**22nd**	twenty-second
23. huszonharmadik	**23rd**	twenty-third
30. harmincadik	**30th**	thirtieth
31. harmincegyedik	**31st**	thirty-first

MAY
3
1998

Brit angol ***British***

3.5.98 3rd May 1998
3/5/98 3 May 1998

Ezerkilencszázkilencvennyolc május harmadika — The third of May nineteen ninety-eight/ May the third, nineteen ninety-eight.

Amerikai angol ***American***

5/3/98 May 3, 1998

Ezerkilencszázkilencvennyolc május harmadika — May third, nineteen ninety-eight.

At the Bank

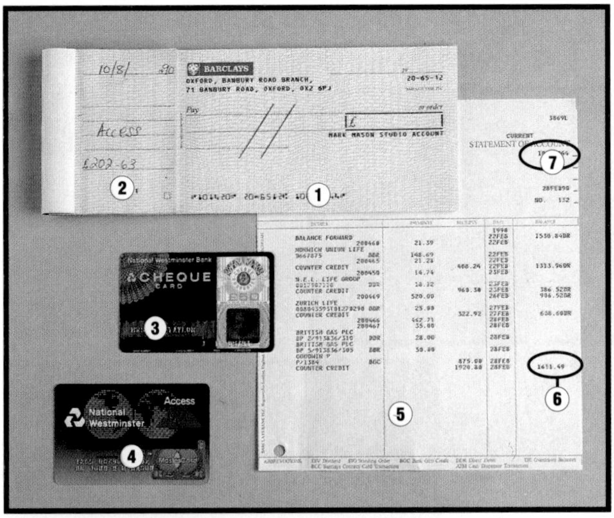
BARCLAYS
National Westminster Bank
CHEQUE CARD
National Westminster
Access
1
2
3
4
5
6
7

14

15
16

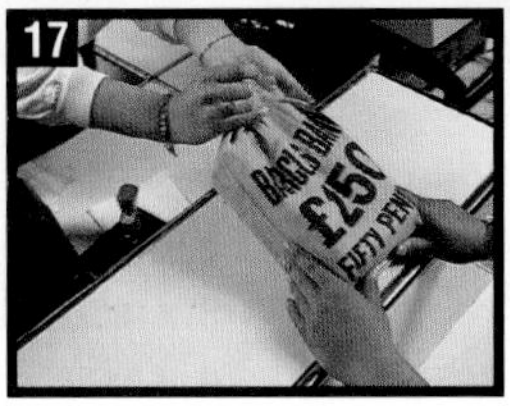
17
£50

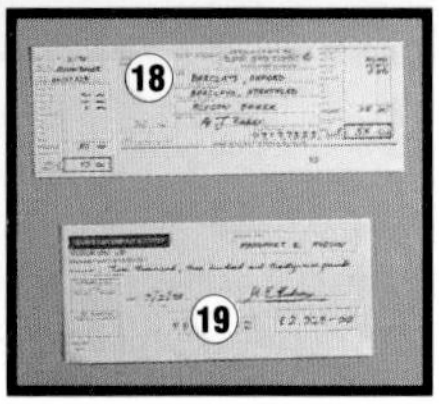
18
19

8
9

10
11
Spread your wings

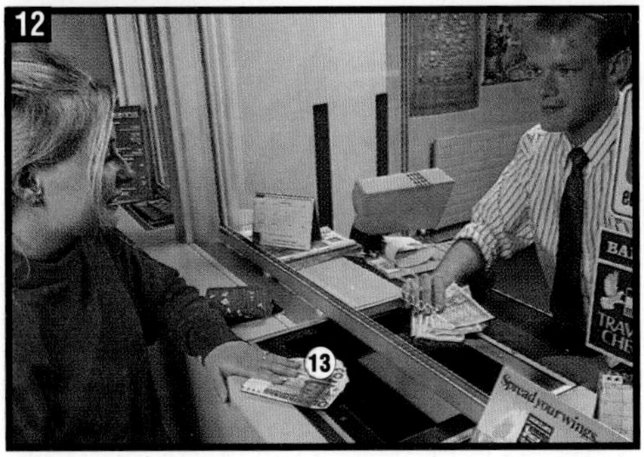
12
13

csekkfüzet	**1**	cheque book (*US* checkbook)
ellenőrzőszelvény	**2**	counterfoil/cheque stub (*US* check stub)
csekk-kártya	**3**	cheque (guarantee) card (*Brit only*)
hitelkártya	**4**	credit card
bankszámlakivonat	**5**	bank statement (*esp US* monthly statement)
egyenleg	**6**	(bank) balance
bankszámlaszám	**7**	(bank) account number
valuta árfolyamok	**8**	exchange rates
pénztáros	**9**	cashier (*US* teller)
utazócsekk-beváltás	**10**	changing a traveller's cheque (*US* cashing a traveler's check)
utazócsekk	**11**	traveller's cheque (*US* traveler's check)
pénzváltás	**12**	changing money
(külföldi) valuta	**13**	foreign currency
csekkbeváltás	**14**	cashing a cheque (*US* cashing a check)
pénzkivétel	**15**	withdrawing cash
bankjegykiadó automata	**16**	cash dispenser/cashpoint (*US* cash machine/ automatic teller)
befizetés	**17**	paying in (*US* making a deposit)
befizetési bizonylat	**18**	paying-in slip (*US* deposit slip)
kifizetési bizonylat	**19**	withdrawal slip

American Money page 35

1
2
3
4
5
1¢/$0.01
5¢/$0.05
10¢/$0.10
25¢/$0.25

érmék	**1**	**coins**
egycentes	**2**	a penny
ötcentes	**3**	a nickel
tízcentes	**4**	a dime
huszonötcentes	**5**	a quarter
bankjegyek	**6**	**bills**
egydolláros (bankjegy)	**7**	a dollar bill
ötdolláros (bankjegy)	**8**	a five dollar bill
tízdolláros (bankjegy)	**9**	a ten dollar bill
húszdolláros (bankjegy)	**10**	a twenty dollar bill
ötvendolláros (bankjegy)	**11**	a fifty dollar bill

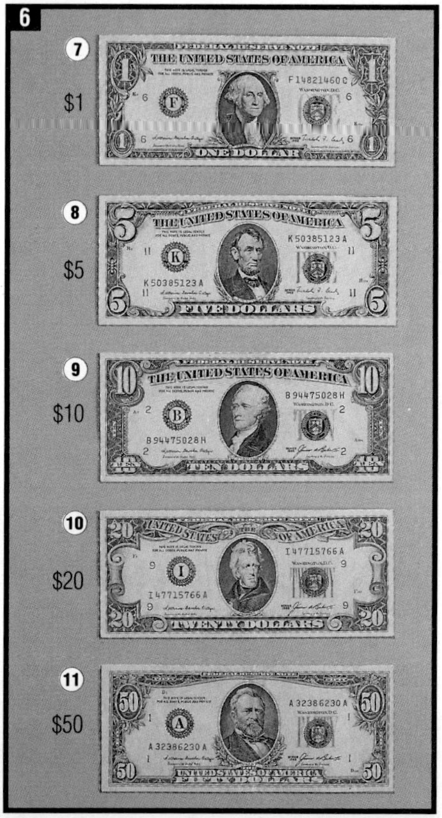
6
7
$1
8
$5
9
$10
10
$20
11
$50

Készpénzfizetés		**Paying (in) cash**
húsz dollár	**12**	twenty dollars
hét dollár (és) kilencvenöt cent/ hét kilencvenöt	**13**	seven dollars and ninety-five cents/ seven ninety-five
blokk/számla	**14**	receipt
összesen	**15**	total
visszajáró pénz	**16**	change

12
$7.95
13
HAPPY BIRTHDAY!

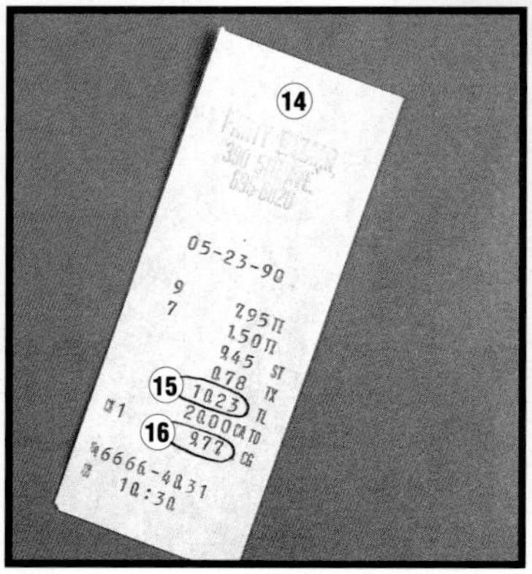
14
05-23-90
15
16

16

British Money

1
2
3
4
5
6
7
8
1p/£0.01
2p/£0.02
5p/£0.05
10p/£0.10
20p/£0.20
50p/£0.50
£1

9
10
£5
11
£10
12
£20
13
£50

érmék **1 coins**
egypennys (érme) **2** a one pence piece/a penny
kétpennys (érme) **3** a two pence piece
ötpennys (érme) **4** a five pence piece
tízpennys (érme) **5** a ten pence piece
húszpennys (érme) **6** a twenty pence piece
ötvenpennys (érme) **7** a fifty pence piece
egyfontos (érme) **8** a pound coin

bankjegyek **9 notes**
ötfontos (bankjegy) **10** a five pound note
tízfontos (bankjegy) **11** a ten pound note
húszfontos (bankjegy) **12** a twenty pound note
ötvenfontos (bankjegy) **13** a fifty pound note

14
£2
18
20p
£3.82
17
10p
50p
15
ORANGE MARMALADE
16

Mennyibe kerül? How much is it?
húsz pennybe (*vagy* húsz penny) **14** twenty pence (*also* 20p)
tíz pennybe (*vagy* tíz penny) **15** ten pence (*also* 10p)
ötven pennybe (*vagy* ötven penny) **16** fifty pence (*also* 50p)
három font nyolcvankét pennybe/ három nyolcvankettőbe **17** three pounds eighty-two pence/ three pounds eighty-two
két fontba **18** two pounds

Time page 37

24 hours = 1 day
7 days = 1 week (wk)
365 days = 1 year (yr)
100 years = 1 century (c)

1
6
7
8
9
10
11
12
13
14

három óra	**1** three o'clock
óralap	**2** clock-face
nagymutató/percmutató	**3** minute-hand
kismutató/óramutató	**4** hour-hand
másodpercmutató	**5** second-hand
kilenc múlt öt perccel/ kilenc óra öt	**6** five past nine (*US also* five after nine)/ nine o five
kilenc múlt tíz perccel	**7** ten past nine (*US also* ten after nine)/ nine ten
negyed tíz	**8** a quarter past nine (*US also* a quarter after nine)/ nine fifteen
fél tíz/kilenc (óra) harminc	**9** half past nine/nine thirty
kilenc (óra) negyven/háromnegyed tíz lesz öt perc múlva	**10** twenty to ten/nine forty
háromnegyed tíz/ kilenc (óra) negyvenöt	**11** a quarter to ten/ nine forty-five
tíz perc múlva tíz (óra)/ kilenc (óra) ötven	**12** ten to ten/nine fifty
tizenkét óra/dél *vagy* éjfel	**13** twelve o'clock/midday (*esp US* noon) *also* midnight
hét perccel múlt tizenkettő/ tizenkettő (óra) hét	**14** seven minutes past twelve (*US also* seven minutes after twelve)/twelve o seven
reggel hét óra	**15** seven am (*US* A.M.)/ seven o'clock in the morning
délután öt óra	**16** five pm (*US* P.M.)/ five o'clock in the afternoon
este nyolc óra	**17** eight pm (*US* P.M.)/ eight o'clock in the evening
éjjel fél tizenkettő	**18** eleven thirty pm (*US* P.M.) half past eleven at night

15
07:00

16
17:00

17
20:00

18
23:30

Emergency Services

Rendőrség	**Police**
rendőrörs	**1** police station
rendőrautó	**2** police car
rendőr	**3** police officer
Tűzoltóság	**Fire Brigade**
	(*US* Fire Department)
tűzoltóautó	**4** fire-engine
létra	**5** ladder
víz	**6** water
füst	**7** smoke
tűz	**8** fire
tűzoltó-készülék	**9** fire extinguisher
tűzoltó	**10** fireman
	(*esp US* fire fighter)
tűzcsap	**11** hydrant
tömlő	**12** hose
Mentők	**Ambulance Service**
autóbaleset	**13** car accident
mentő(autó)	**14** ambulance
sérült (személy)	**15** injured man
hordágy	**16** stretcher
mentős	**17** paramedic
nemzetközi hívószám	**18** international code
országhívószám	**19** country code
körzethívószám	**20** area code
telefonszám	**21** (tele)phone number
telefonfülke	**22** (tele)phone box
	(*esp US* telephone booth)
telefonkagyló	**23** receiver
telefonkártya	**24** phonecard (*Brit only*)
nyílás	**25** slot
tárcsa	**26** dial

1
2
3

7
8
5
6
4
ABBEY NATIONAL

9

10
H
11
12

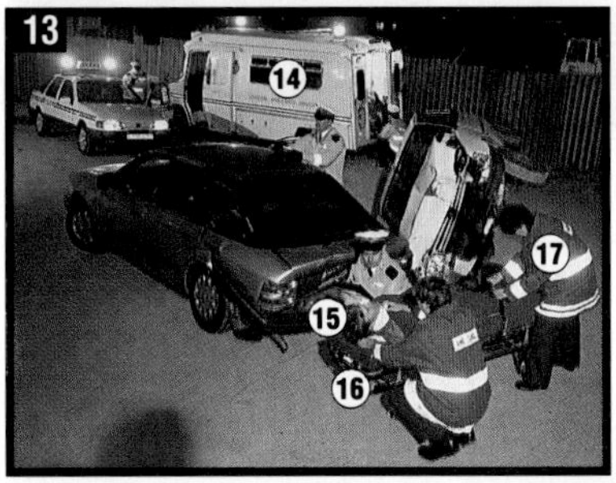
13
14
17
15
16

(18) (19)
00 44 865 56767
0865 56767
(20) (21)

In Britain the telephone number for the police, fire and ambulance services is 999. In the US the emergency number is 911.

Nagy-Britanniában a rendőrség, a tűzoltóság és a mentők telefonszáma 999.
Az USA-ban a segélykérő szám 911.

Telephone
Phonecard
22
22

23

24

25

26

Jobs 1 page 39

(festő)művész **1** artist
kertész **2** gardener
lemezlovas **3** disc jockey (*US* disk jockey)
rádió/TV-bemondó **4** newsreader (*esp US* newscaster)

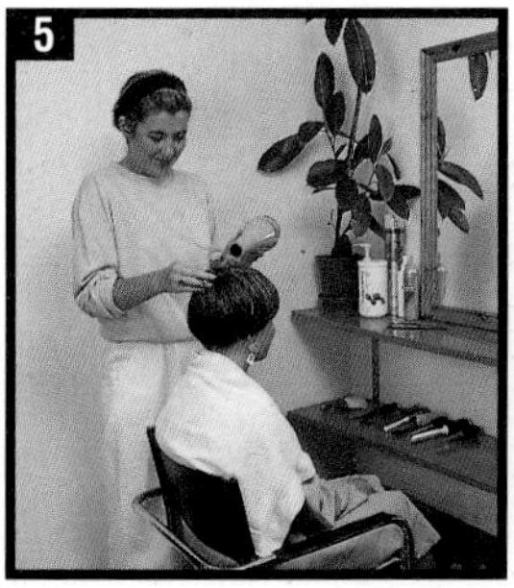
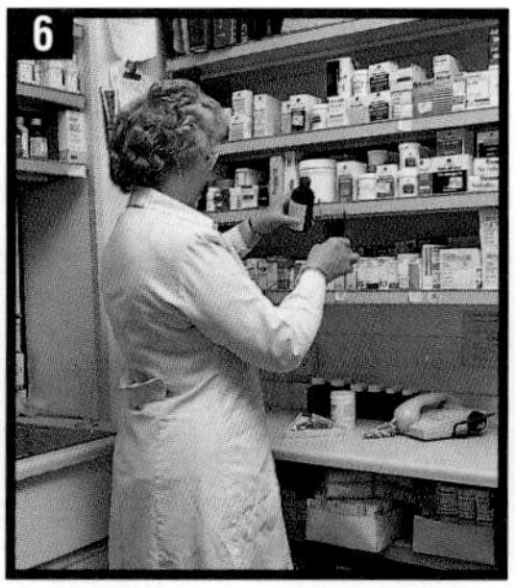

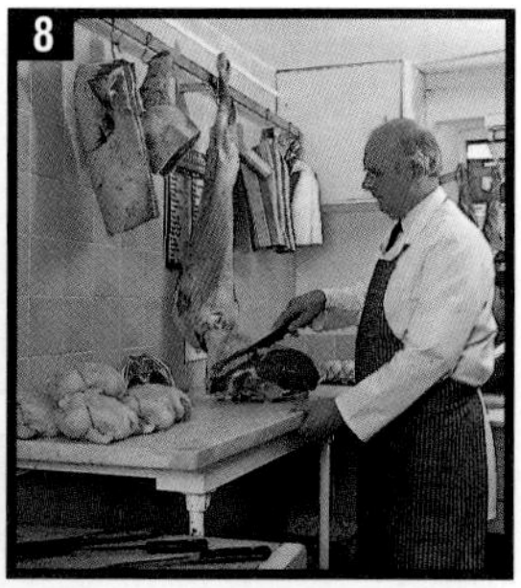

fodrász **5** hairdresser
gyógyszerész **6** pharmacist
pék **7** baker
hentes **8** butcher

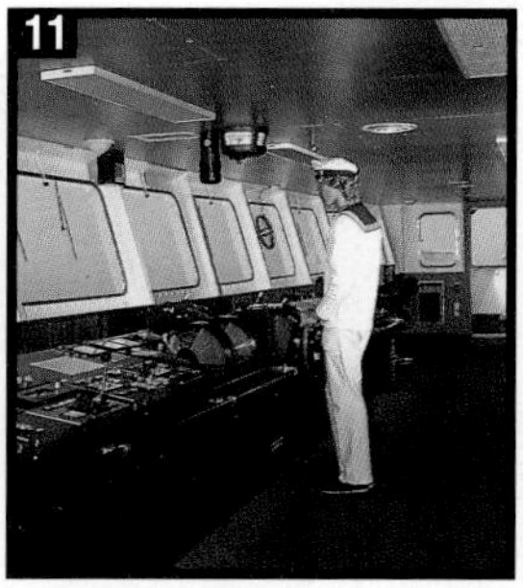

paraszt/gazdálkodó **9** farmer
halász **10** fisherman
tengerész **11** sailor
katona **12** soldier

Jobs 2

1

2
PLANT &
TRANSPORT

3
PARIS

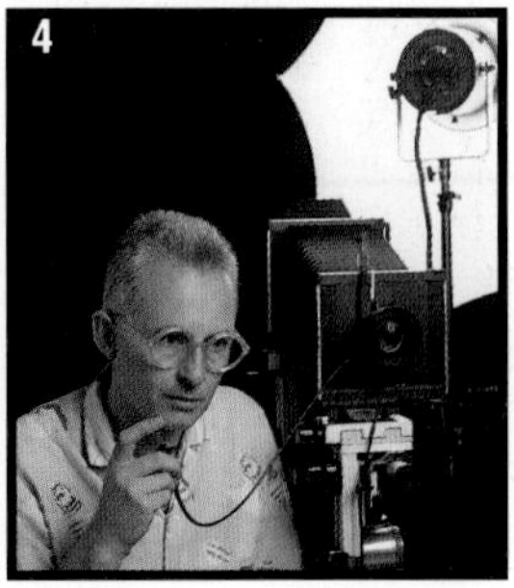
4

építész **1** architect
teherautó-vezető **2** lorry driver (*US* truck driver)
utazási ügynök **3** travel agent
fényképész/fotós **4** photographer

5

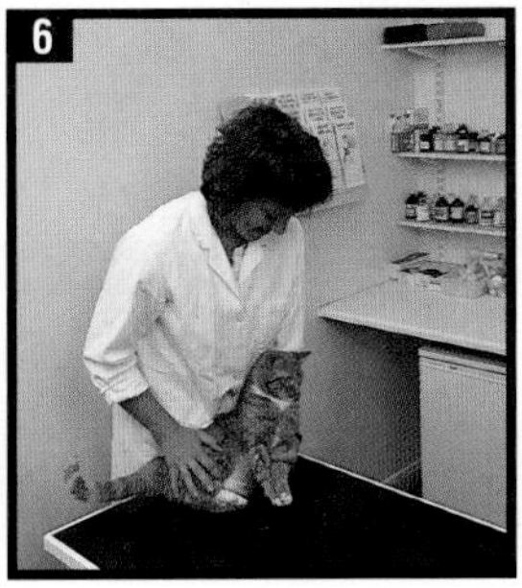
6

7

8

számítógép-programozó **5** computer programmer
állatorvos **6** vet
villanyszerelő **7** electrician
ács **8** carpenter

9

10

11

12

hegesztő(munkás) **9** welder
víz- és gáz(vezeték)szerelő **10** plumber
(gép)szerelő **11** mechanic
kőműves **12** bricklayer

Daily Routine page 41

1
07:00

2

3

4
07:05

Felébred. **1** He wakes up.
Felkel/Kiszáll az ágyból. **2** He gets up/He gets out of bed.
Lemegy a földszintre. **3** He goes downstairs.
Kocogni megy/Futni megy. **4** He goes jogging.

5
07:25

6

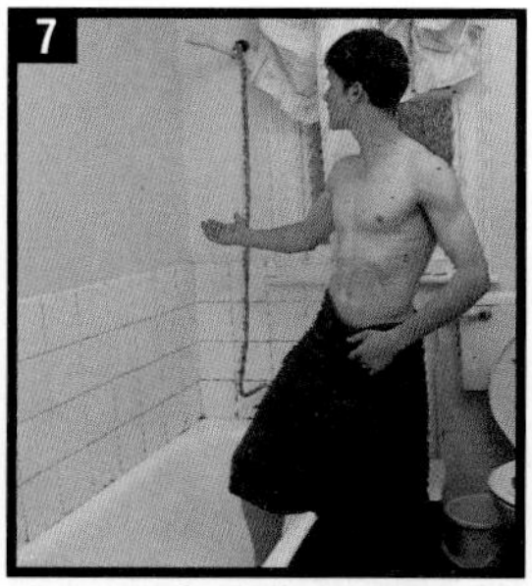
7

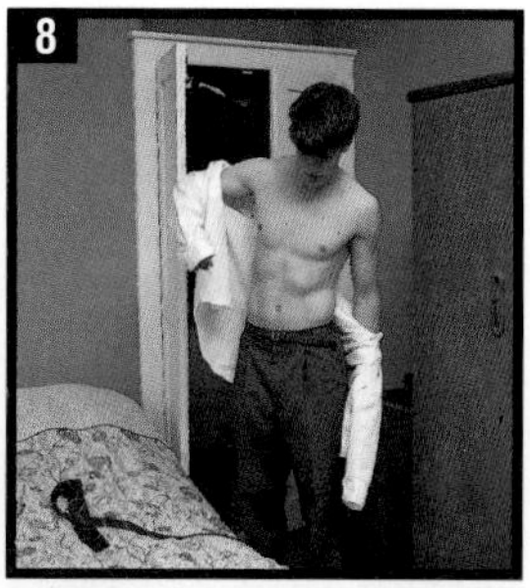
8

Visszajön. **5** He comes back.
Összeszedi a postát/leveleket. **6** He picks up the post (*US* mail).
(Le)zuhanyozik. **7** He has a shower.
(*esp US* He takes a shower.)
(Fel)öltözik. **8** He gets dressed.

9
07:40

10
07:50

11

12
SPORTS

Reggelizik/Megeszi a reggelit. **9** He has breakfast/He eats breakfast.
Elmegy hazulról. **10** He leaves home.
Újságot vesz. **11** He buys a newspaper.
Zenét hallgat. **12** He listens to music.

page 42

Daily Routine 2

13
08:15

14

15
09:00

16
11:00

Elkapja a vonatot/Felszáll a vonatra. **13** He catches the train.
Olvassa az újságot. **14** He reads the newspaper.
Elkezdi a munkát. **15** He starts work.
Iszik egy (csésze) kávét/Kávézik. **16** He has a cup of coffee.
He drinks some coffee.

17
13:00

18
17:00

19
SPORTS CENTRE

20

Ebédel/Megeszi az ebédet. **17** He has lunch/He eats lunch.
Befejezi a munkát. **18** He finishes work.
A sporttelepre hajt. **19** He drives to the sports centre (*US* health club).
Találkozik a barátaival. **20** He meets his friends.

21

22
20:00

23

24
23:30

Squasht játszik. **21** He plays squash.
Vacsorázik/Megeszi a vacsorát. **22** He has dinner/He eats dinner.
Televíziót/tévét néz. **23** He watches television/TV.
Lefekszik (aludni). **24** He goes to bed.

Office Verbs page 43

1
2

3

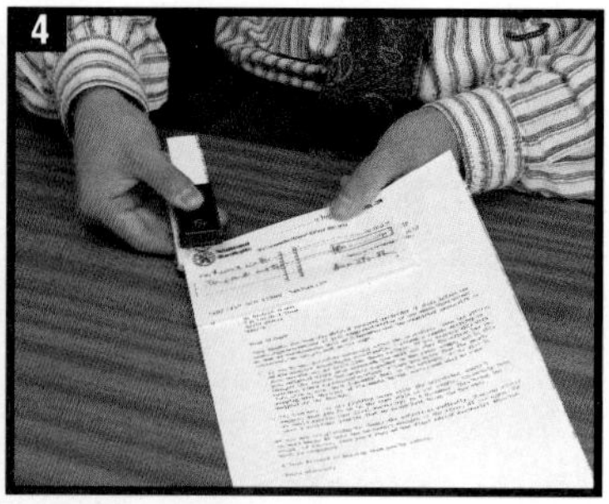
4

Levelet diktál.	**1** She is dictating a letter.
diktafon	**2** Dictaphone/dictating machine
Levelet gépel.	**3** He is typing a letter.
Gépel.	He is typing.
Csekket kapcsol egy levélhez.	**4** He is stapling a cheque to a letter. (*US* check)

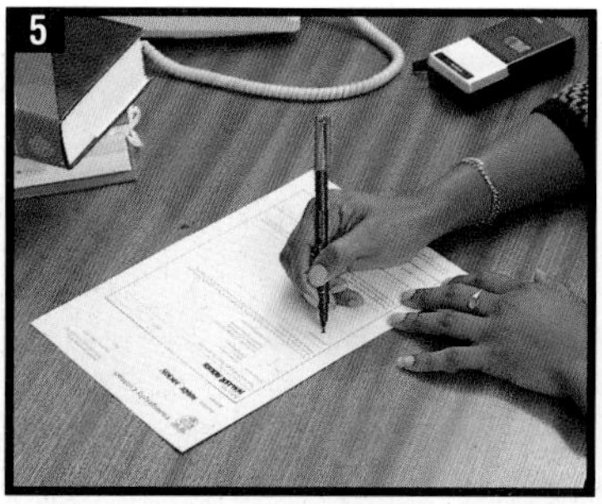
5

6
7

8

Kitölt egy űrlapot.	**5** She is filling in a form.
	(*US* She is filling out a form.)
Aláír egy levelet.	**6** She is signing a letter.
aláírás	**7** signature
Bejegyez egy megbeszélést/találkozót.	**8** She is making a note of an appointment.

9

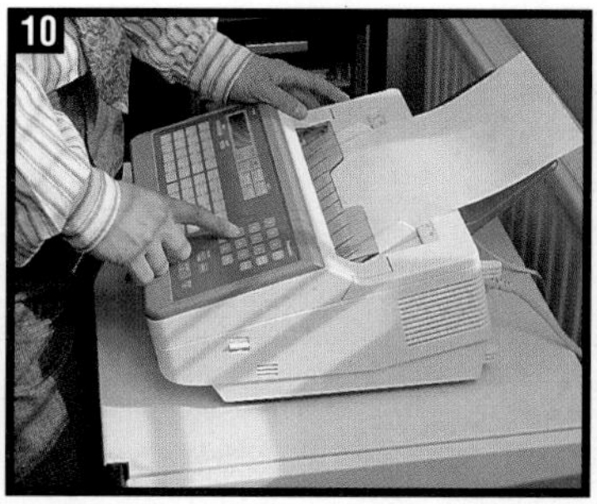
10

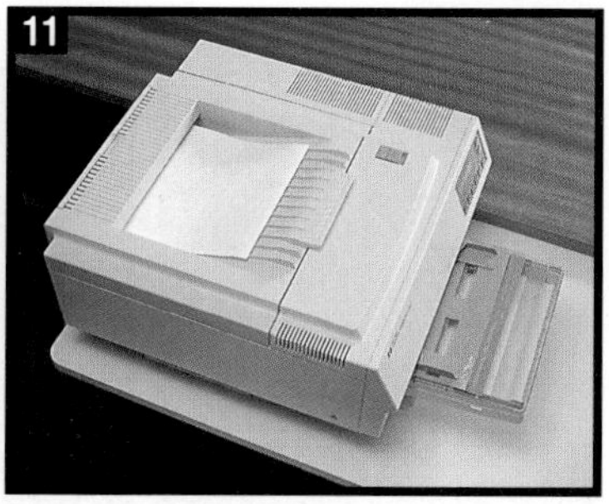
11

Iktat.	**9** He is filing.
(Tele)faxot küld.	**10** He is sending a fax.
Faxol egy levelet.	He is faxing a letter.
(Ki)nyomtat.	**11** It is printing.
Kinyomtat egy példányt.	**12** It is printing a copy.

The Office

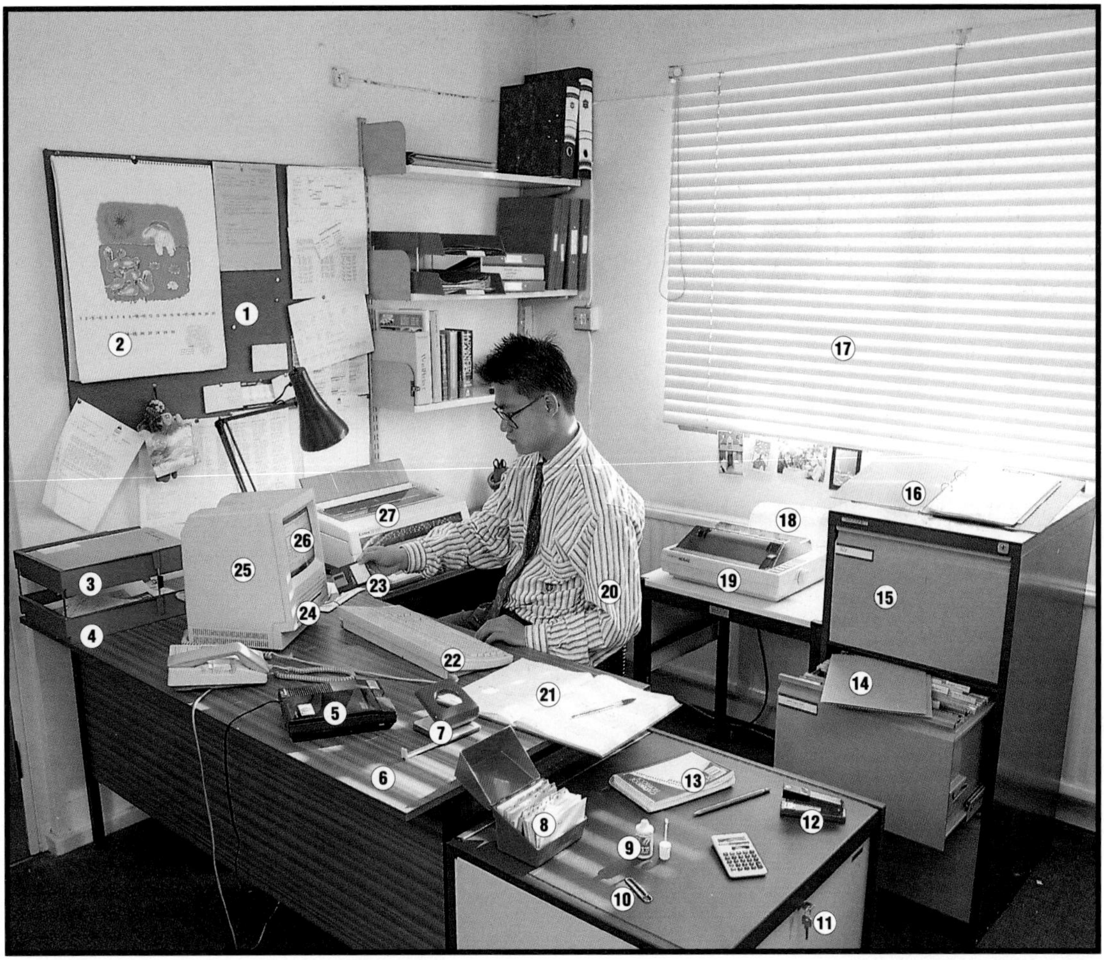
1
2
3
4
5
6
7
8
9
10
11
12
13
14
15
16
17
18
19
20
21
22
23
24
25
26
27

falitábla	**1**	notice-board (*US* bulletin board)
naptár	**2**	calendar
"elintézendő ügyek" tálca	**3**	in-tray (*US* in box)
"elintézett ügyek" tálca	**4**	out-tray (*US* out box)
üzenetrögzítős telefon	**5**	answering machine (*Brit also* answerphone)
íróasztal	**6**	desk
lyukasztó	**7**	hole-punch
kártyaindex	**8**	card index (*US* card file)
korrektor (folyadék)	**9**	Tipp-Ex (*esp US* correction fluid)
gemkapocs	**10**	paper-clip
kulcs	**11**	key
tűzőgép	**12**	stapler
jegyzetfüzet	**13**	notebook
akta	**14**	file
iratszekrény	**15**	filing cabinet (*US* file cabinet)
kapcsos iratrendező	**16**	ring binder
reluxa/lécroletta	**17**	venetian blind
(a) kinyomtatott szöveg	**18**	printout
nyomtató	**19**	printer
titkár(nő)	**20**	secretary
előjegyzési naptár	**21**	diary (*US* appointment book)
billentyűzet	**22**	keyboard
floppy disk	**23**	floppy disk
disk drive	**24**	disk drive
személyi számítógép	**25**	personal computer/PC
képernyő	**26**	screen
írógép	**27**	typewriter

A Science Laboratory 1 page 45

1
2
3
4
5
6
7
8
9
10
11
12
13
14
15
16
17
18
19
20
21
22
23
24
25
26

védőszemüveg	**1** goggles	fecskendő	**16** syringe
kémcső	**2** test-tube	Ellenmeyer-lombik	**17** conical flask
láng	**3** flame	U-cső	**18** U-tube
gumicső	**4** rubber tubing	zsámoly	**19** stool
Bunsen-égő	**5** Bunsen burner	Bunsen-állvány	**20** clamp stand (*US* ring stand)
(kémcső)állvány	**6** rack	hőmérő	**21** thermometer
mozsártörő	**7** pestle	gömblombik	**22** round bottom flask
dörzsmozsár	**8** mortar	hűtő	**23** condenser
állólombik	**9** flat bottom flask	főzőpohár	**24** measuring beaker (*US* graduated beaker)
tölcsér	**10** funnel	azbeszt-lángelosztó	**25** gauze (*US* wire mesh screen)
szűrőpapír	**11** filter paper	vasháromláb	**26** tripod
prizma	**12** prism		
fogócsipesz	**13** tongs		
nagyító(üveg)	**14** magnifying glass		
fecskendődugattyú	**15** plunger		

page 46

A Science Laboratory 2

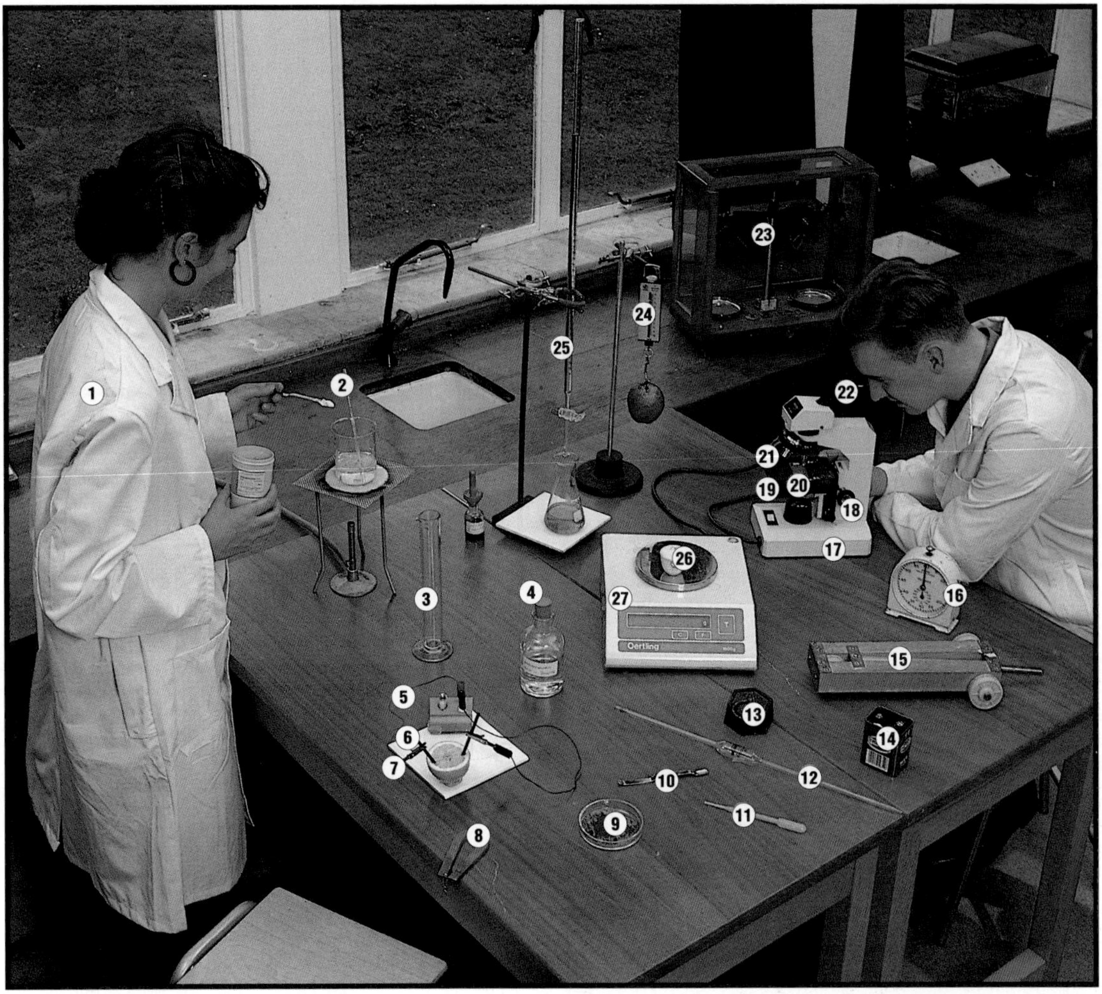

laboratóriumi köpeny	**1**	lab coat
üvegpálca	**2**	glass rod
mérőhenger	**3**	measuring cylinder (*US* graduated cylinder)
dugasz	**4**	stopper
vezeték	**5**	wire
elektróda	**6**	electrode
krokodilcsipesz	**7**	crocodile clip (*US* alligator clip)
mágnes(patkó)	**8**	magnet
Petri-csésze	**9**	Petri dish (*US* petri dish)
spatula	**10**	spatula
cseppentő	**11**	dropper
pipetta	**12**	pipette
súly	**13**	weight
elem	**14**	battery
kiskocsi	**15**	trolley (*US* cart)
stopperóra	**16**	stop clock (*US* timer)
mikroszkóp	**17**	microscope
fókuszszabályozó	**18**	focusing control (*US also* focusing knob)
tárgyasztal	**19**	stage
lemez	**20**	slide
tárgylencse	**21**	objective lens
szemlencse	**22**	eyepiece
mérleg	**23**	balance/scales (*US* scale)
rugós erőmérő	**24**	spring balance
büretta	**25**	burette
olvasztótégely	**26**	crucible
mikromérleg	**27**	microbalance

Shapes and Lines page 47

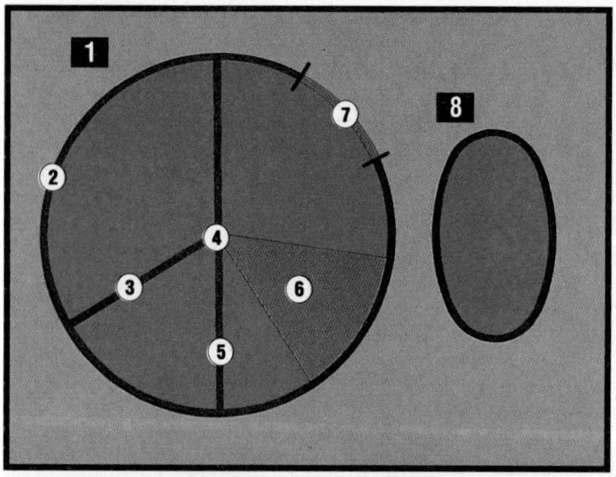
1
2
3
4
5
6
7
8

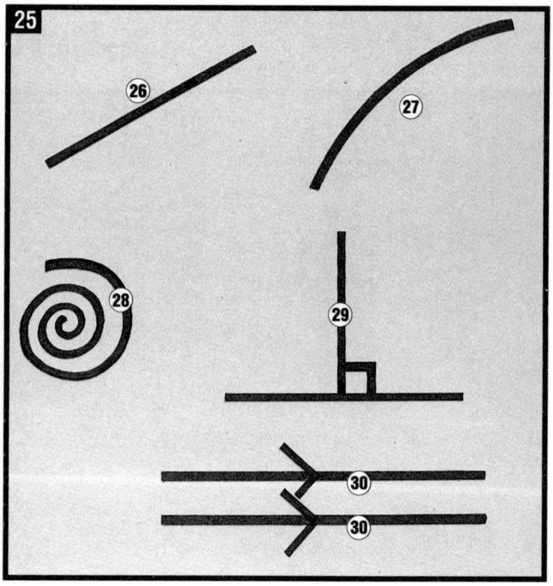
25
26
27
28
29
30
30

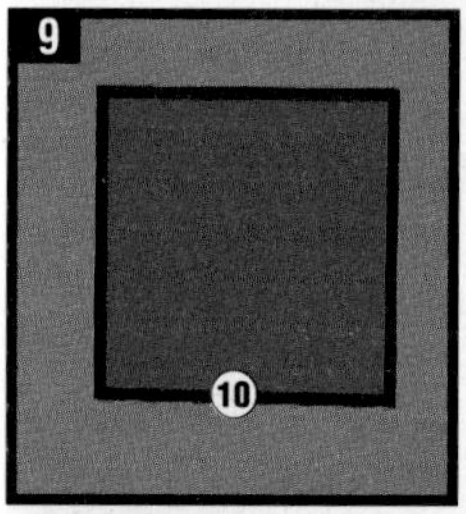
9
10

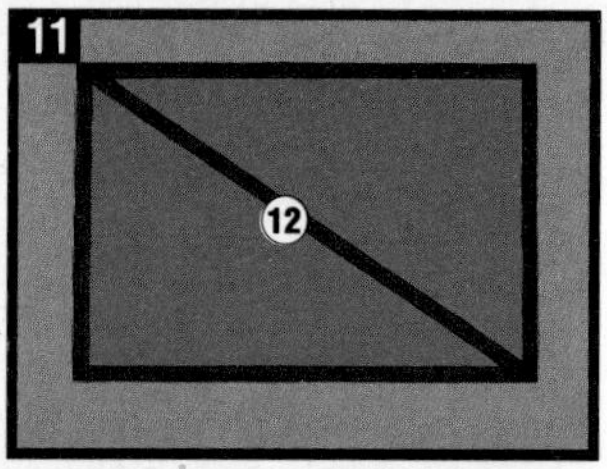
11
12

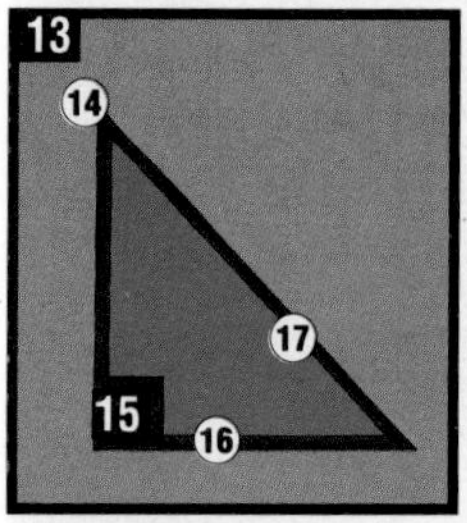
13
14
15
16
17

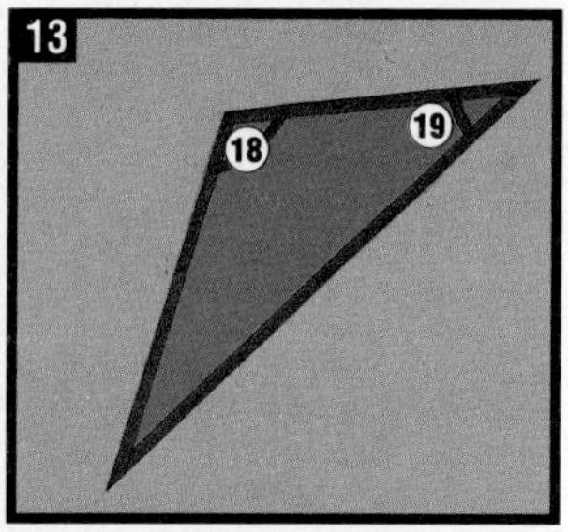
13
18
19

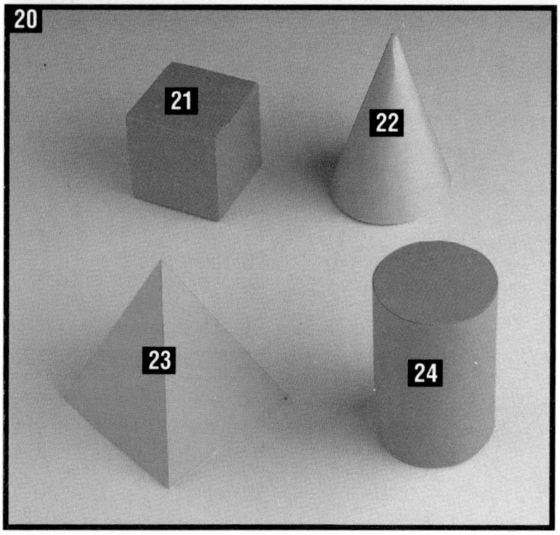
20
21
22
23
24

kör	**1** circle
kerület	**2** circumference
sugár	**3** radius
középpont	**4** centre (*US* center)
átmérő	**5** diameter
körcikk	**6** sector
körív	**7** arc
ovális	**8** oval
négyzet	**9** square
oldal	**10** side
téglalap	**11** rectangle
átló	**12** diagonal
háromszög	**13** triangle
csúcs	**14** apex
derékszög	**15** right angle
alap	**16** base
átfogó	**17** hypotenuse
tompaszög	**18** obtuse angle
hegyesszög	**19** acute angle
térformák/testek	**20** solid figures
kocka	**21** cube
kúp	**22** cone
gúla	**23** pyramid
henger	**24** cylinder
vonalak	**25** lines
egyenes (vonal)	**26** straight line
görbe (vonal)	**27** curve
spirális (vonal)	**28** spiral
függőleges/merőleges (vonal)	**29** perpendicular line
párhuzamosok/párhuzamos vonalak	**30** parallel lines

Measurement

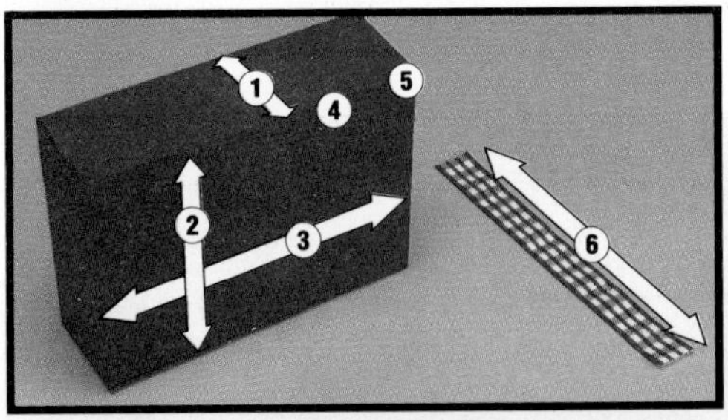
1
2
3
4
5
6

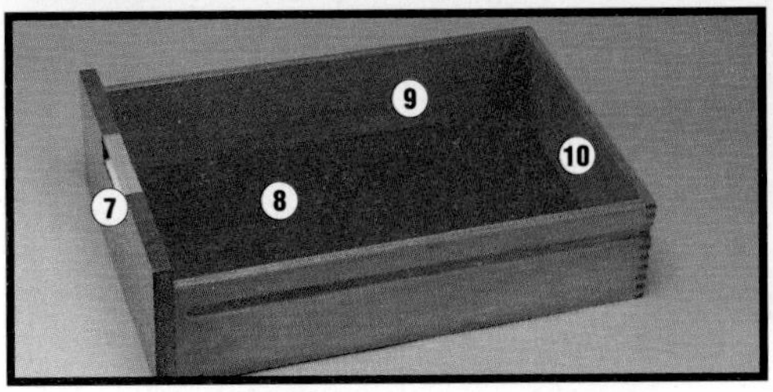
7
8
9
10

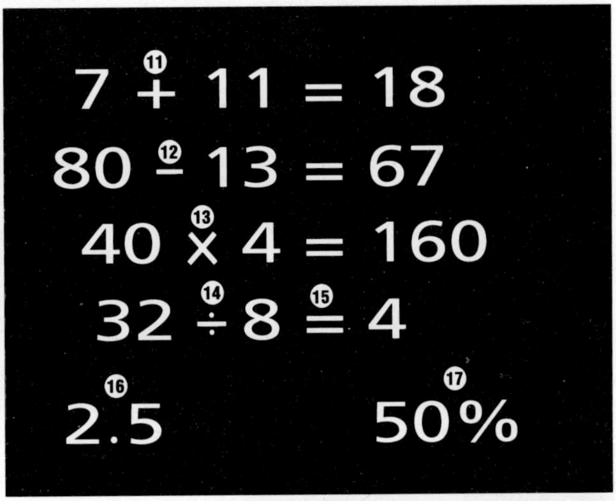
7 + 11 = 18 (11)
80 − 13 = 67 (12)
40 × 4 = 160 (13)
32 ÷ 8 = 4 (14) (15)
2.5 (16)
50% (17)

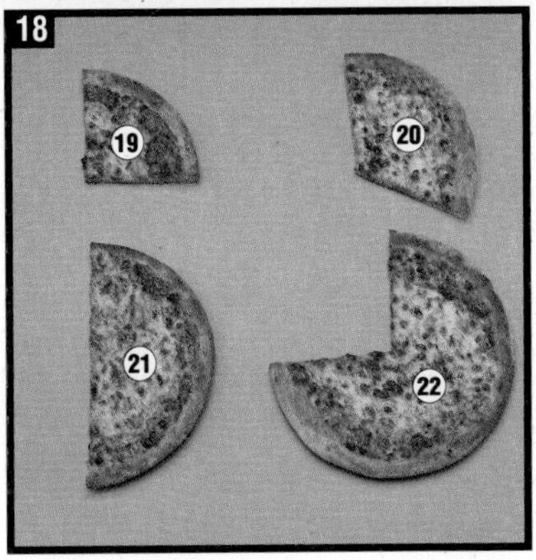
18
19
20
21
22

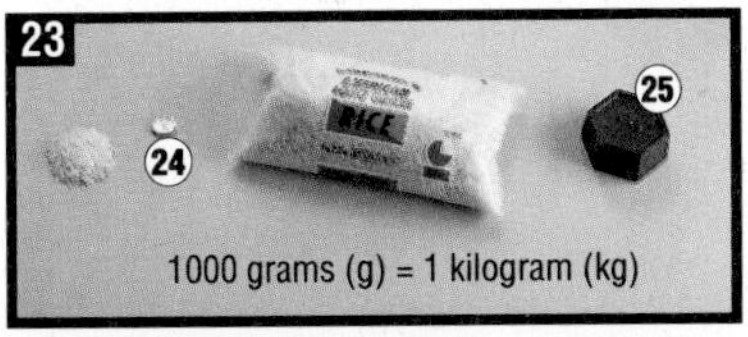
23
24
25
RICE
1000 grams (g) = 1 kilogram (kg)

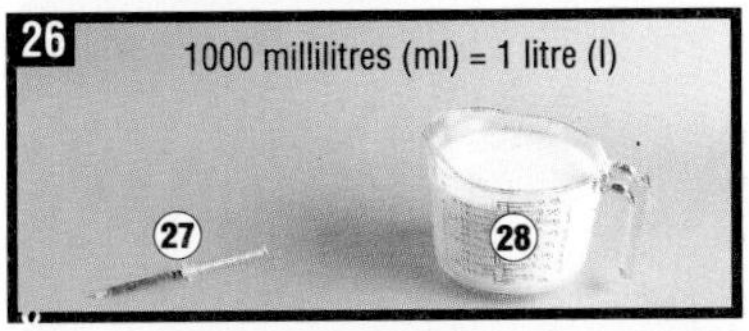
26
1000 millilitres (ml) = 1 litre (l)
27
28

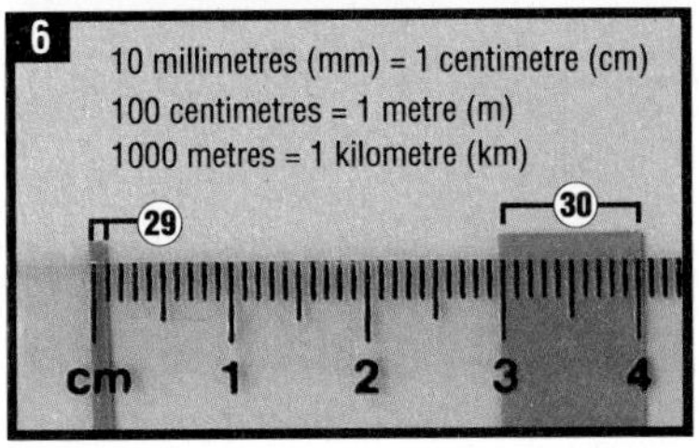
6
10 millimetres (mm) = 1 centimetre (cm)
100 centimetres = 1 metre (m)
1000 metres = 1 kilometre (km)
29
30
cm 1 2 3 4

mélység **1** depth
magasság **2** height
szélesség **3** width
él **4** edge
sarok **5** corner
hosszúság **6** length
eleje (valaminek) **7** front
alja (valaminek) **8** bottom
oldala (valaminek) **9** side
hátulja (valaminek) **10** back
plusz/meg **11** plus
mínusz/-ból, -ből **12** minus
szorozva x-val, -vel **13** multiplied by/times
osztva x-val, -vel **14** divided by
egyenlő **15** equals
kettő egész öt tized **16** two point five
ötven százalék **17** fifty per cent
törtszámok **18** fractions
negyed/ $^1/_4$ **19** a quarter/ $^1/_4$
harmad/ $^1/_3$ **20** a third/ $^1/_3$
fél/ $^1/_2$ **21** a half/ $^1/_2$
háromnegyed/ $^3/_4$ **22** three quarters/ $^3/_4$
súly **23** weight
10 gramm **24** 10 grams*
kilo(gramm) **25** kilogram*
térfogat **26** capacity
milliliter **27** millilitre (*US* milliliter)*
liter **28** litre (*US* liter)*
milliméter **29** millimetre (*US* millimeter)*
centiméter **30** centimetre (*US* centimeter)*

Ezek a mértékegységek általában nem használatosak az amerikai angolban.

**These measurements are not usually used in US English.*

The Classroom page 49

20th July
Maths
Topic
of the future
The Golden Key
Reading
Sewing
1
2
3
4
5
6
7
8
9
10
11
12
13
14
15
16
17
18

tábla	**1** blackboard (*US also* chalkboard)
tanuló/diák	**2** pupil (*esp US* student)
tankönyv	**3** textbook
füzet	**4** exercise book (*US* notebook)
zsebszámológép	**5** calculator
háromszögű vonalzó	**6** set square (*US* triangle)
szögmérő	**7** protractor
iskolatáska	**8** school bag
(csempe)padló	**9** (tiled) floor
szék	**10** chair
földgömb	**11** globe
olló	**12** scissors
festőállvány	**13** easel
ecset	**14** paintbrush
festékkészlet	**15** paintbox
tanár	**16** teacher
kép	**17** picture
térkép	**18** map

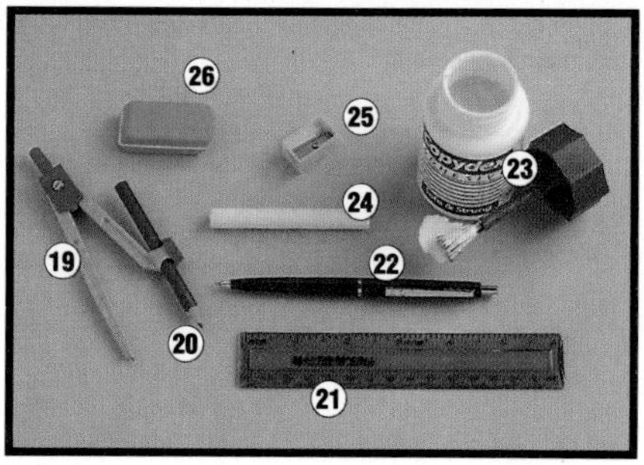

19
20
21
22
23
24
25
26

körző	**19** (pair of) compasses (*also* compass)
ceruza	**20** pencil
vonalzó	**21** ruler
toll	**22** pen
ragasztó	**23** glue
(egy darab) kréta	**24** (piece of) chalk
ceruzahegyező	**25** pencil-sharpener
radír(gumi)	**26** rubber (*US* eraser)

page 50

Space

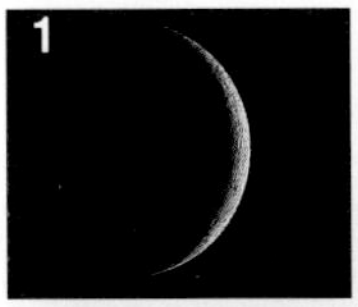
1

2

3

4

5
6
7
8

9

10
11
12

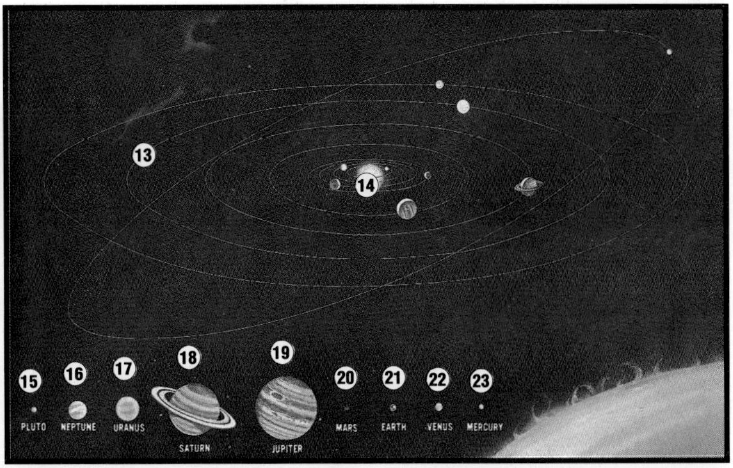
13
14
15
16
17
18
19
20
21
22
23
PLUTO
NEPTUNE
URANUS
SATURN
JUPITER
MARS
EARTH
VENUS
MERCURY

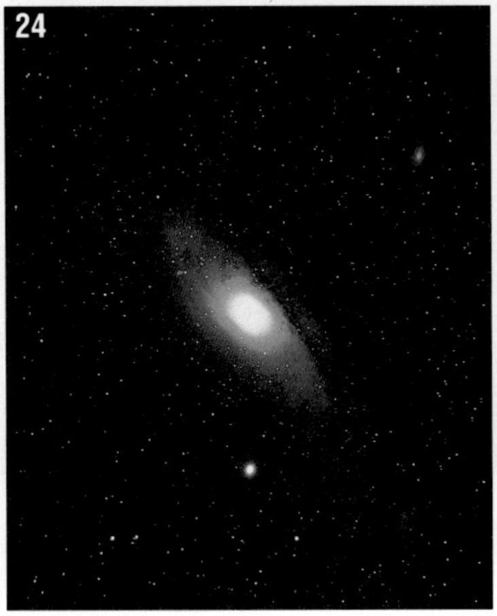
24

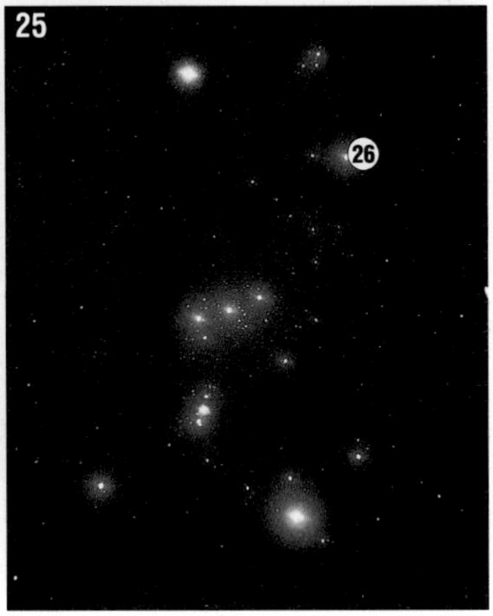
25
26

újhold	**1** new moon (*esp US* crescent moon)
félhold/első negyed	**2** half moon (*US also* first quarter)
telihold	**3** full moon
fogyó hold/utolsó negyed	**4** old moon (*US* half moon/last quarter)
holdkomp	**5** lunar module
asztronauta/űrhajós	**6** astronaut
űrruha	**7** spacesuit
holdjáró	**8** lunar vehicle
műhold	**9** satellite
rakéta	**10** rocket
űrhajó	**11** space shuttle
kilövőállás	**12** launch pad

A Naprendszer	**The Solar System**
körpálya	**13** orbit
Nap	**14** Sun
A bolygók	**The Planets**
Plútó	**15** Pluto
Neptunusz	**16** Neptune
Uránusz	**17** Uranus
Szaturnusz	**18** Saturn
Jupiter	**19** Jupiter
Mars	**20** Mars
Föld	**21** Earth
Vénusz	**22** Venus
Merkur	**23** Mercury
A világűr	**Outer Space**
csillagrendszer	**24** galaxy
csillagkép	**25** constellation
csillag	**26** star

The Weather page 51

1

2

3
4

5

Süt a nap. **1** It's sunny.
Esik az eső/Esős az idő. **2** It's raining. (*US also* It's rainy.)
Havazik/Esik a hó. **3** It's snowing. (*US also* It's snowy.)
hó **4** snow
Fúj a szél. **5** It's windy.

6

7

8

9

Párás az idő. **6** It's misty.
Ködös az idő. **7** It's foggy.
Felhős az idő. **8** It's cloudy.
Viharos az idő. **9** It's stormy.

10
11

12

13

14

zivatar **10** thunderstorm
villám(lás) **11** lightning
szivárvány **12** rainbow
Ragyogó napsütés van. **13** It's bright.
Borús az idő. **14** It's dull. (*US* It's dark.)

page 52

The Temperature
The Seasons

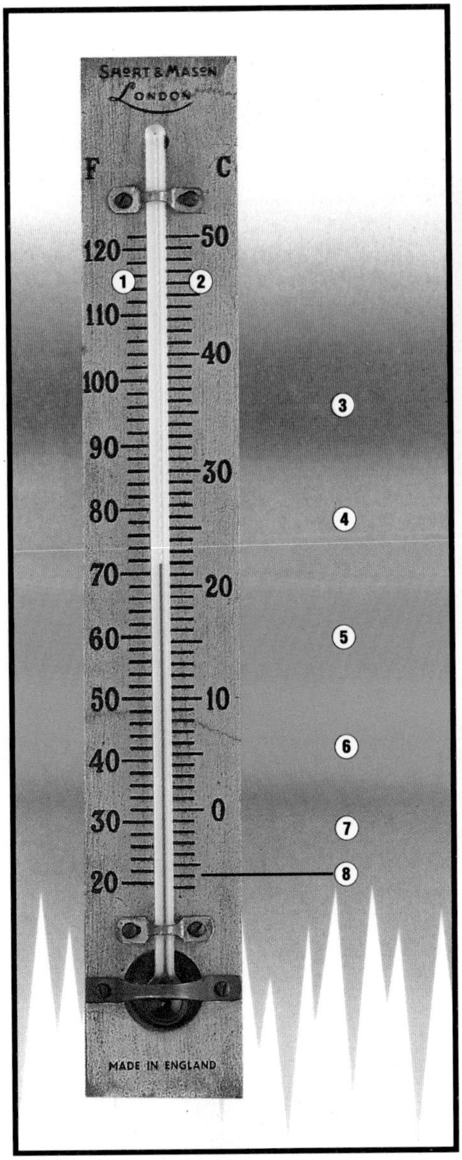

SHORT & MASON
LONDON
F
C
120
110
100
90
80
70
60
50
40
30
20
50
40
30
20
10
0
1
2
3
4
5
6
7
8
MADE IN ENGLAND

9

10

11

12

A hőmérséklet	The Temperature
Fahreinheit-fokok	**1** degrees Fahrenheit
Celsius-fokok	**2** degrees Celsius (*or* centigrade)
Hőség van.	**3** It's hot.
Meleg van.	**4** It's warm.
Hűvös van.	**5** It's cool.
Hideg van.	**6** It's cold.
Fagy (van).	**7** It's freezing.
Mínusz hat fok van.	**8** It's minus six (degrees). (*US* It's six (degrees) below zero.)

Az évszakok	The Seasons
tavasszal	**9** in (the) spring
nyáron	**10** in (the) summer
ősszel	**11** in (the) autumn (*US* in the fall)
télen	**12** in (the) winter

A hónapok	The Months
január	January
február	February
március	March
április	April
május	May
június	June
július	July
augusztus	August
szeptember	September
október	October
november	November
december	December

The World page 53

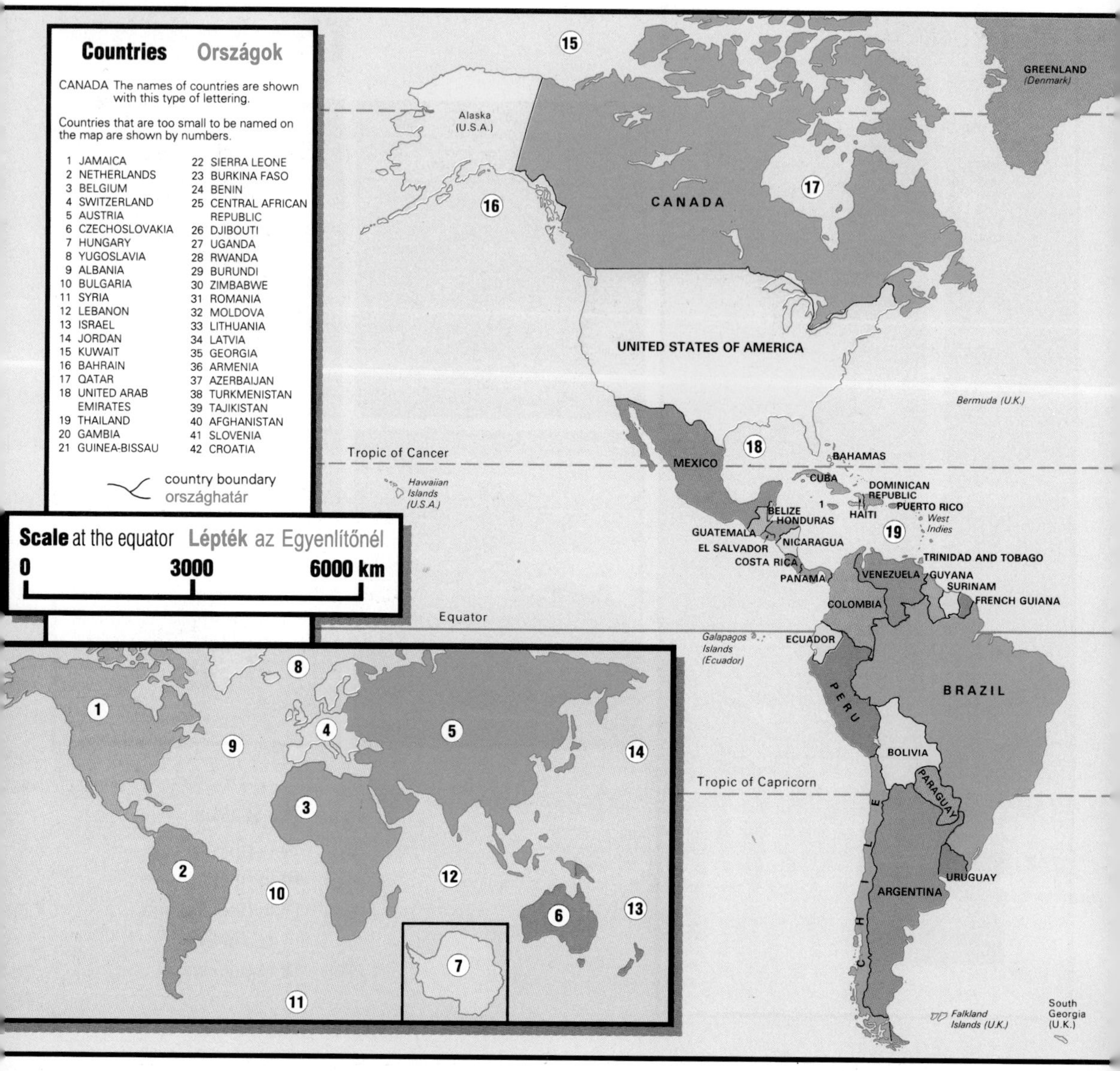
Countries Országok
CANADA The names of countries are shown with this type of lettering.
Countries that are too small to be named on the map are shown by numbers.
1 JAMAICA
2 NETHERLANDS
3 BELGIUM
4 SWITZERLAND
5 AUSTRIA
6 CZECHOSLOVAKIA
7 HUNGARY
8 YUGOSLAVIA
9 ALBANIA
10 BULGARIA
11 SYRIA
12 LEBANON
13 ISRAEL
14 JORDAN
15 KUWAIT
16 BAHRAIN
17 QATAR
18 UNITED ARAB EMIRATES
19 THAILAND
20 GAMBIA
21 GUINEA-BISSAU
22 SIERRA LEONE
23 BURKINA FASO
24 BENIN
25 CENTRAL AFRICAN REPUBLIC
26 DJIBOUTI
27 UGANDA
28 RWANDA
29 BURUNDI
30 ZIMBABWE
31 ROMANIA
32 MOLDOVA
33 LITHUANIA
34 LATVIA
35 GEORGIA
36 ARMENIA
37 AZERBAIJAN
38 TURKMENISTAN
39 TAJIKISTAN
40 AFGHANISTAN
41 SLOVENIA
42 CROATIA
country boundary
országhatár
Scale at the equator Lépték az Egyenlítőnél
0 3000 6000 km
15
GREENLAND (Denmark)
Alaska (U.S.A.)
16
17
CANADA
UNITED STATES OF AMERICA
Bermuda (U.K.)
Tropic of Cancer
18
BAHAMAS
MEXICO
Hawaiian Islands (U.S.A.)
CUBA
DOMINICAN REPUBLIC
1
BELIZE
HONDURAS
HAITI
PUERTO RICO
West Indies
GUATEMALA
19
EL SALVADOR
NICARAGUA
COSTA RICA
TRINIDAD AND TOBAGO
PANAMA
VENEZUELA
GUYANA
SURINAM
FRENCH GUIANA
COLOMBIA
Equator
Galapagos Islands (Ecuador)
ECUADOR
BRAZIL
PERU
BOLIVIA
Tropic of Capricorn
PARAGUAY
CHILE
URUGUAY
ARGENTINA
Falkland Islands (U.K.)
South Georgia (U.K.)
8
1
9
4
5
14
3
2
10
12
6
13
7
11

Kontinensek	**Continents**
Észak-Amerika	**1** North America
Dél-Amerika	**2** South America
Afrika	**3** Africa
Európa	**4** Europe
Ázsia	**5** Asia
Ausztrália	**6** Australia
Antarktisz	**7** Antarctica
Óceánok	**Oceans**
Északi-Jeges-tenger	**8** Arctic
Atlanti-óceán	**9** North Atlantic
Atlanti-óceán	**10** South Atlantic
Déli-Jeges-tenger	**11** Antarctic
Indiai-óceán	**12** Indian
Csendes-óceán	**13** South Pacific
Csendes-óceán	**14** North Pacific
Tengerek és (tenger)öblök	**Seas, Gulfs, and Bays**
Beaufort-tenger	**15** Beaufort Sea
Alaszkai-öböl	**16** Gulf of Alaska
Hudson-öböl	**17** Hudson Bay
Mexikói-öböl	**18** Gulf of Mexico
Karib-tenger	**19** Caribbean Sea

The World

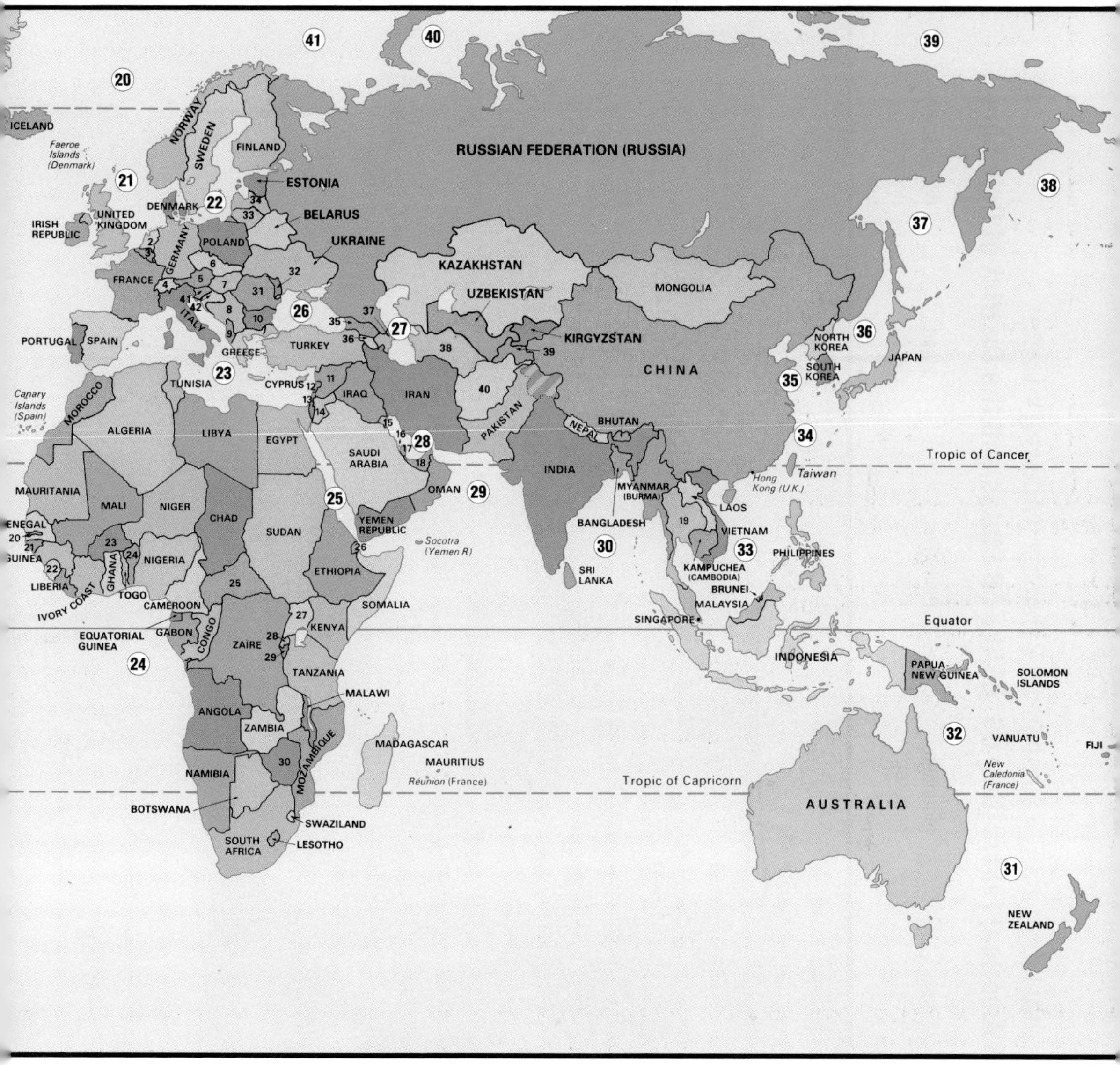
41
40
39
20
ICELAND
Faeroe Islands (Denmark)
21
NORWAY
SWEDEN
FINLAND
RUSSIAN FEDERATION (RUSSIA)
38
ESTONIA
DENMARK
22
34
33
BELARUS
37
UNITED KINGDOM
IRISH REPUBLIC
POLAND
GERMANY
UKRAINE
KAZAKHSTAN
FRANCE
32
31
MONGOLIA
UZBEKISTAN
26
ITALY
10
27
35
37
36
KIRGYZSTAN
NORTH KOREA
36
PORTUGAL
SPAIN
GREECE
TURKEY
38
39
JAPAN
23
TUNISIA
CYPRUS
IRAQ
IRAN
40
CHINA
SOUTH KOREA
35
Canary Islands (Spain)
MOROCCO
ALGERIA
LIBYA
EGYPT
PAKISTAN
NEPAL
BHUTAN
28
34
SAUDI ARABIA
Tropic of Cancer
INDIA
Hong Kong (U.K.)
Taiwan
MAURITANIA
OMAN
29
MYANMAR (BURMA)
MALI
NIGER
CHAD
25
LAOS
SENEGAL
SUDAN
YEMEN REPUBLIC
BANGLADESH
VIETNAM
GUINEA
NIGERIA
GHANA
Socotra (Yemen R)
30
33
PHILIPPINES
ETHIOPIA
SRI LANKA
KAMPUCHEA (CAMBODIA)
LIBERIA
IVORY COAST
TOGO
BRUNEI
CAMEROON
SOMALIA
MALAYSIA
SINGAPORE
KENYA
Equator
EQUATORIAL GUINEA
GABON
CONGO
ZAIRE
24
INDONESIA
TANZANIA
PAPUA-NEW GUINEA
SOLOMON ISLANDS
MALAWI
ANGOLA
ZAMBIA
32
VANUATU
FIJI
MOZAMBIQUE
MADAGASCAR
MAURITIUS
Réunion (France)
NAMIBIA
New Caledonia (France)
Tropic of Capricorn
BOTSWANA
AUSTRALIA
SWAZILAND
SOUTH AFRICA
LESOTHO
31
NEW ZEALAND

Norvég-tenger	**20**	Norwegian Sea
Északi-tenger	**21**	North Sea
Balti-tenger	**22**	Baltic Sea
Földközi-tenger	**23**	Mediterranean Sea
Guineai-öböl	**24**	Gulf of Guinea
Vörös-tenger	**25**	Red Sea
Fekete-tenger	**26**	Black Sea
Kaszpi-tenger	**27**	Caspian Sea
Perzsa-öböl	**28**	The Gulf
Arab-tenger	**29**	Arabian Sea
Bengáli-öböl	**30**	Bay of Bengal
Tasman-tenger	**31**	Tasman Sea
Korall-tenger	**32**	Coral Sea
Dél-kínai-tenger	**33**	South China Sea
Kelet-kínai-tenger	**34**	East China Sea
Sárga-tenger	**35**	Yellow Sea
Japán-tenger	**36**	Sea of Japan
Ohotszki-tenger	**37**	Sea of Okhotsk
Bering-tenger	**38**	Bering Sea
Laptyev-tenger	**39**	Laptev Sea
Kara-tenger	**40**	Kara Sea
Barents-tenger	**41**	Barents Sea

The USA

page 55

(Amerikai) Egyesült Államok (*röv.* USA) = 50 állam és Columbia (választó) körzete

the United States (of America) (*abbrs* (the) US, USA) = 50 States and the District of Columbia

state line	államhatár
lake	tó
mountain	hegység
main river	főfolyó
island	sziget
• city *or* town	nagyváros *vagy* város

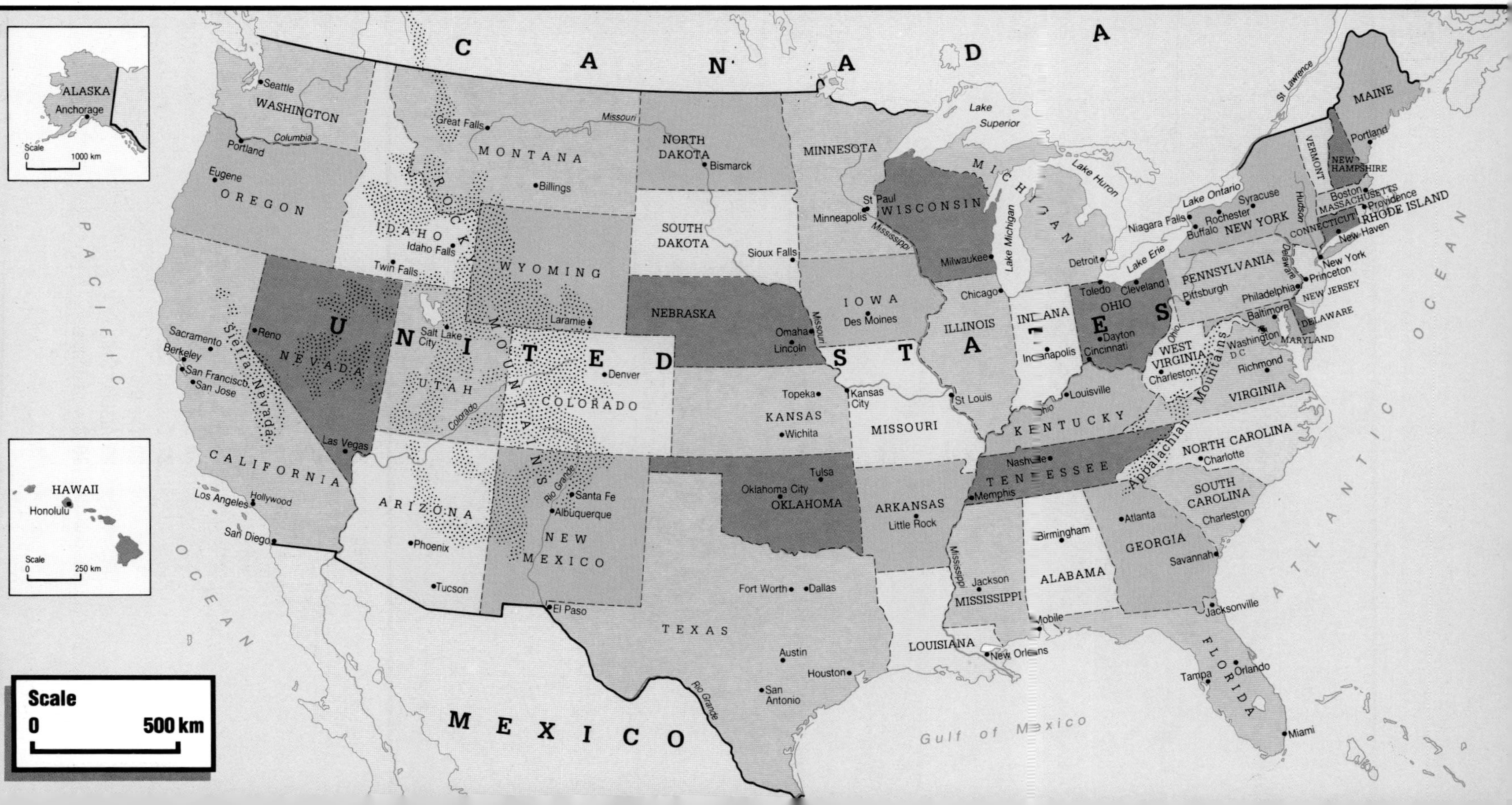
CANADA
UNITED STATES
MEXICO
PACIFIC OCEAN
ATLANTIC OCEAN
Gulf of Mexico
ALASKA
Anchorage
Scale 0 1000 km
HAWAII
Honolulu
Scale 0 250 km
Scale 0 500 km
WASHINGTON
Seattle
Columbia
OREGON
Portland
Eugene
CALIFORNIA
Sacramento
Berkeley
San Francisco
San Jose
Los Angeles
Hollywood
San Diego
Sierra Nevada
NEVADA
Reno
Las Vegas
IDAHO
Idaho Falls
Twin Falls
MONTANA
Great Falls
Billings
Missouri
ROCKY MOUNTAINS
WYOMING
Laramie
UTAH
Salt Lake City
Colorado
ARIZONA
Phoenix
Tucson
COLORADO
Denver
NEW MEXICO
Santa Fe
Albuquerque
Rio Grande
El Paso
NORTH DAKOTA
Bismarck
SOUTH DAKOTA
Sioux Falls
NEBRASKA
Omaha
Lincoln
KANSAS
Topeka
Wichita
Kansas City
OKLAHOMA
Oklahoma City
Tulsa
TEXAS
Fort Worth
Dallas
Austin
Houston
San Antonio
MINNESOTA
St Paul
Minneapolis
Mississippi
IOWA
Des Moines
MISSOURI
St Louis
ARKANSAS
Little Rock
LOUISIANA
New Orleans
WISCONSIN
Milwaukee
Lake Superior
Lake Michigan
Lake Huron
Lake Erie
Lake Ontario
MICHIGAN
Detroit
ILLINOIS
Chicago
INDIANA
Indianapolis
OHIO
Toledo
Cleveland
Dayton
Cincinnati
Ohio
KENTUCKY
Louisville
TENNESSEE
Nashville
Memphis
MISSISSIPPI
Jackson
ALABAMA
Birmingham
Mobile
GEORGIA
Atlanta
Savannah
FLORIDA
Jacksonville
Orlando
Tampa
Miami
SOUTH CAROLINA
Charleston
NORTH CAROLINA
Charlotte
Appalachian Mountains
VIRGINIA
Richmond
WEST VIRGINIA
Charleston
Washington DC
MARYLAND
Baltimore
DELAWARE
NEW JERSEY
Princeton
PENNSYLVANIA
Pittsburgh
Philadelphia
Delaware
NEW YORK
New York
Buffalo
Niagara Falls
Rochester
Syracuse
Hudson
CONNECTICUT
New Haven
RHODE ISLAND
Providence
MASSACHUSETTS
Boston
VERMONT
NEW HAMPSHIRE
MAINE
Portland
St Lawrence

The British Isles

international boundary

national boundary

boundaries of districts in Northern Ireland, counties in the Irish Republic, England and Wales, and regions and island areas in Scotland

● capital city

• city *or* town

Scale
0 75 150 km

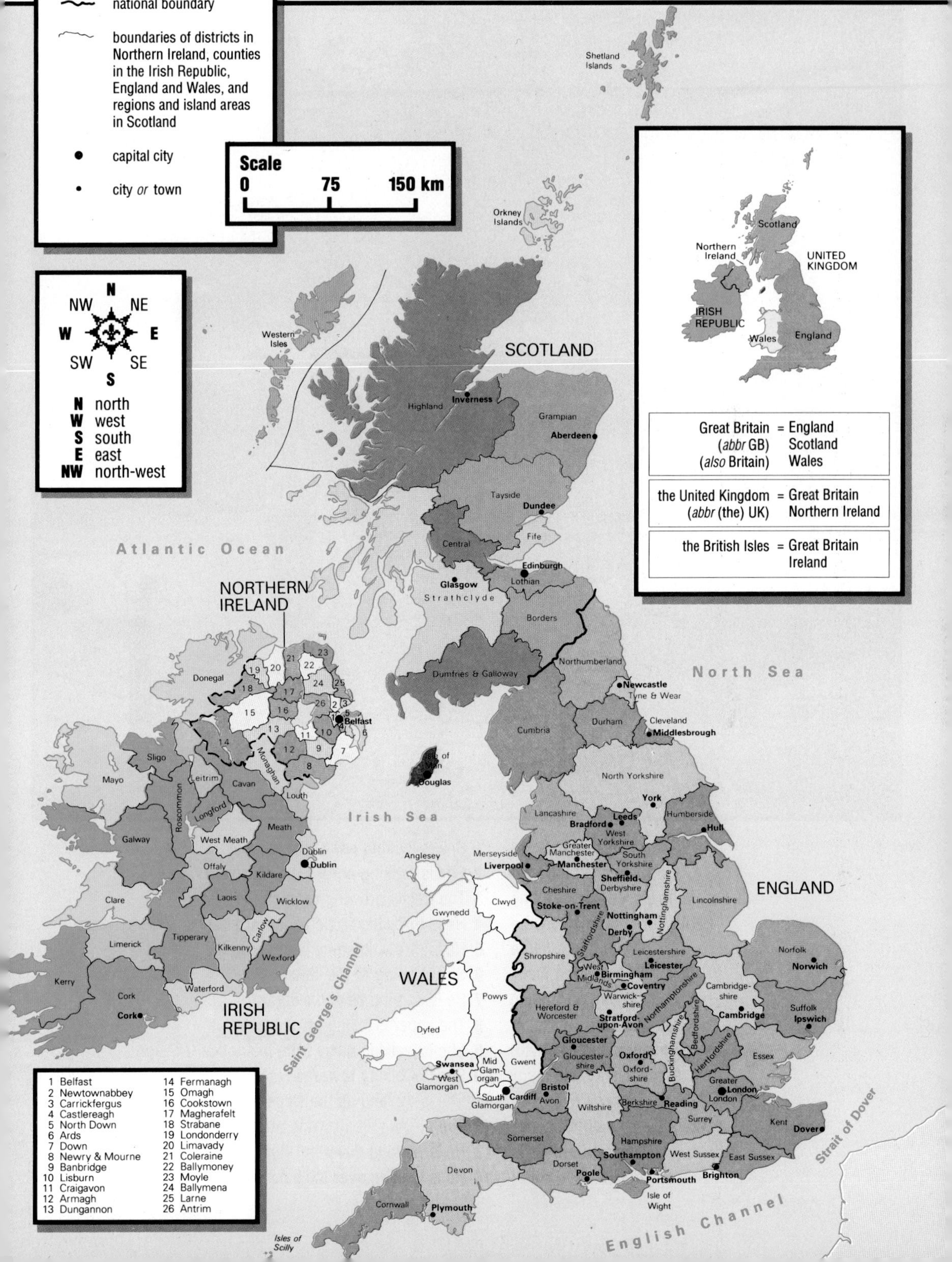

N
NW
NE
W
E
SW
SE
S
N north
W west
S south
E east
NW north-west
Shetland Islands
Orkney Islands
Western Isles
SCOTLAND
Highland
Inverness
Grampian
Aberdeen
Tayside
Dundee
Fife
Central
Edinburgh
Lothian
Glasgow
Strathclyde
Borders
Dumfries & Galloway
Atlantic Ocean
North Sea
NORTHERN IRELAND
Donegal
Belfast
Sligo
Mayo
Leitrim
Cavan
Monaghan
Louth
Roscommon
Longford
Meath
Galway
West Meath
Dublin
Offaly
Kildare
Laois
Wicklow
Clare
Limerick
Tipperary
Carlow
Kilkenny
Wexford
Kerry
Waterford
Cork
IRISH REPUBLIC
Isle of Man
Douglas
Irish Sea
Northumberland
Newcastle
Tyne & Wear
Cumbria
Durham
Cleveland
Middlesbrough
North Yorkshire
York
Lancashire
Leeds
Bradford
West Yorkshire
Humberside
Hull
Merseyside
Liverpool
Greater Manchester
Manchester
South Yorkshire
Sheffield
Derbyshire
Nottinghamshire
Lincolnshire
ENGLAND
Anglesey
Gwynedd
Clwyd
Cheshire
Stoke-on-Trent
Staffordshire
Nottingham
Derby
Shropshire
Leicestershire
Leicester
Norfolk
Norwich
West Midlands
Birmingham
Coventry
Warwickshire
Northamptonshire
Cambridgeshire
Cambridge
Suffolk
Ipswich
WALES
Powys
Hereford & Worcester
Stratford-upon-Avon
Bedfordshire
Buckinghamshire
Hertfordshire
Essex
Dyfed
Saint George's Channel
Gloucester
Gloucestershire
Oxford
Oxfordshire
Swansea
West Glamorgan
Mid Glamorgan
Gwent
South Glamorgan
Cardiff
Bristol
Avon
Wiltshire
Berkshire
Reading
Greater London
London
Surrey
Kent
Dover
Strait of Dover
Somerset
Hampshire
West Sussex
East Sussex
Southampton
Devon
Dorset
Poole
Portsmouth
Brighton
Isle of Wight
Cornwall
Plymouth
Isles of Scilly
English Channel
Scotland
Northern Ireland
UNITED KINGDOM
IRISH REPUBLIC
Wales
England

Great Britain (*abbr* GB) (*also* Britain)	=	England Scotland Wales
the United Kingdom (*abbr* (the) UK)	=	Great Britain Northern Ireland
the British Isles	=	Great Britain Ireland

1 Belfast	14 Fermanagh
2 Newtownabbey	15 Omagh
3 Carrickfergus	16 Cookstown
4 Castlereagh	17 Magherafelt
5 North Down	18 Strabane
6 Ards	19 Londonderry
7 Down	20 Limavady
8 Newry & Mourne	21 Coleraine
9 Banbridge	22 Ballymoney
10 Lisburn	23 Moyle
11 Craigavon	24 Ballymena
12 Armagh	25 Larne
13 Dungannon	26 Antrim

Prepositions 1 page 57

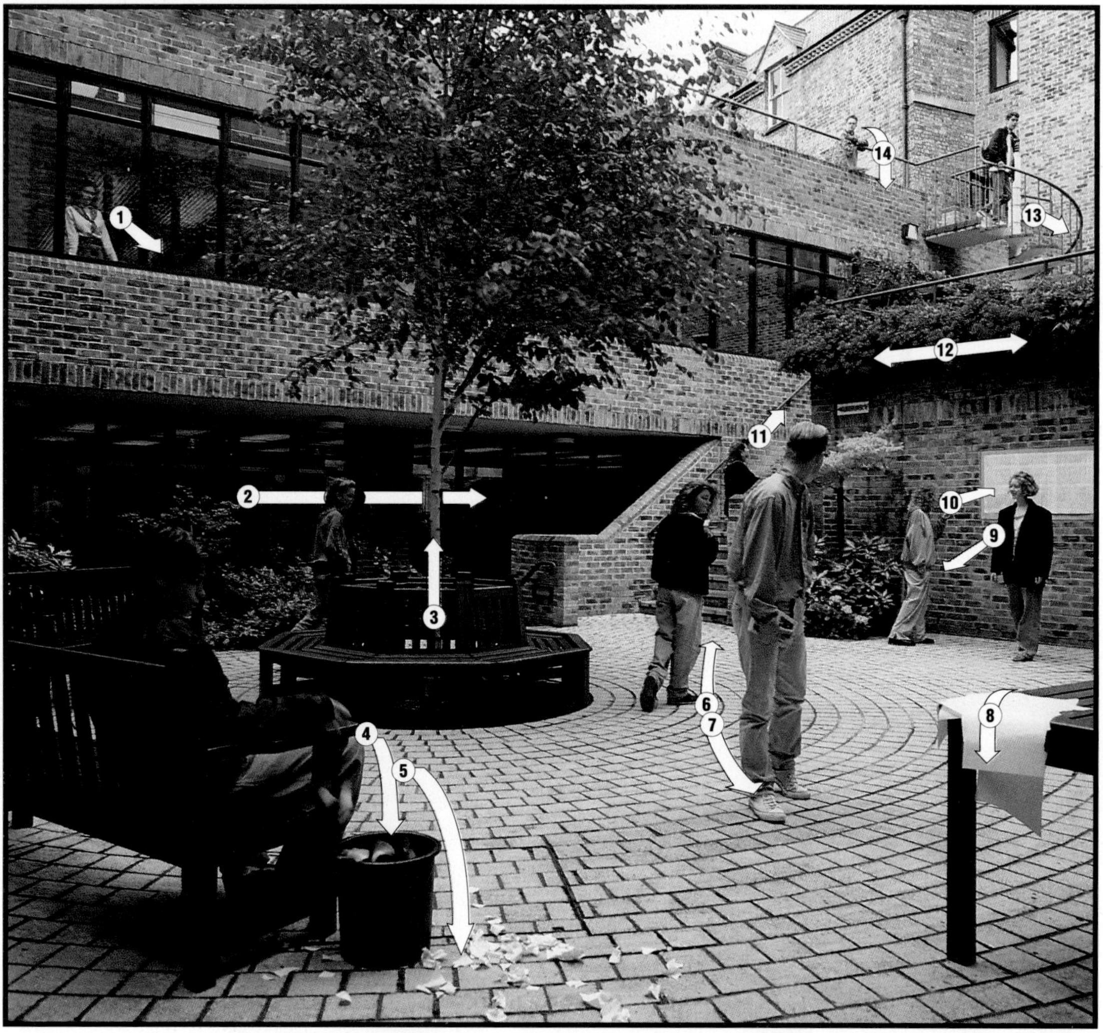

Kinéz az ablakon.	**1** She is looking **out of** the window.
Átmegy az udvaron.	**2** She is walking **across** the courtyard.
A fa az ülésen **keresztül** nő.	**3** The tree is growing **through** the seat.
Papírt dob a szemétkosárba.	**4** He is throwing some paper **into** the bin (*US* trash can).
Papírt dob a földre.	**5** He is throwing some paper **onto** the ground.
A könyvtárba megy.	**6** She is going **to** the library.
A könyvtárból jön.	**7** He is coming **from** the library.
A papír leesik az asztalról.	**8** The paper is falling **off** the table.
Elmegy a hirdetménytől.	**9** She is walking **away from** the notice (*US* sign).
A hirdetmény **felé** megy.	**10** She is walking **towards** (*esp US* **toward**) the notice (*US* sign).
Felmegy a lépcsőn.	**11** She is walking **up** the steps.
A virágok a fal **mentén** nőnek.	**12** The flowers are growing **along** the wall.
Lemegy a lépcsőn.	**13** He is walking **down** the steps.
Átnéz az erkély(korlát) **fölött**.	**14** He is looking **over** the balcony.

page 58

Prepositions 2

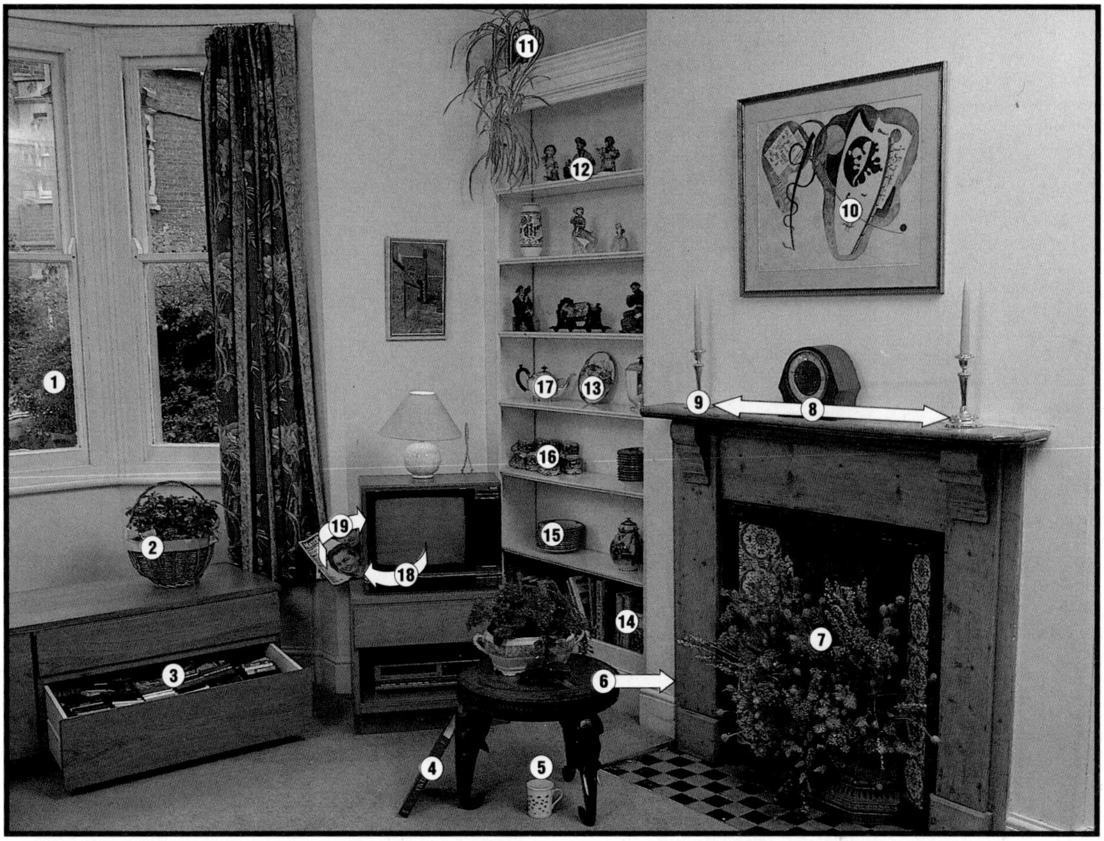
1
2
3
4
5
6
7
8
9
10
11
12
13
14
15
16
17
18
19

A bokor az ablak**on kívül** van.	**1** The bush is **outside** the window.
A szalag a kosár **körül** van.	**2** The ribbon is **round** the basket (*esp US* **around** the basket).
A kazetták a fiók**ban** vannak.	**3** The cassettes are **in/inside** the drawer.
A könyvet **neki**támasztották az asztal**nak**.	**4** The book is **against** the table.
A bögre az asztal **alatt** van.	**5** The mug is **under/underneath** the table.
Az asztal **közel** van a kandalló**hoz**.	**6** The table is **by/nea**r the fireplace.
A szárazvirágok a kandalló**ban** vannak.	**7** The dried flowers are **in** the fireplace.
Az óra a gyertyák **között** van.	**8** The clock is **between** the candles.
A gyertya a kandallópárkány**on** van.	**9** The candle is **on** the mantelpiece (*US* mantel).
A kép a kandallópárkány **fölött** van.	**10** The picture is **over** the mantelpiece (*US* mantel).
A növény **a** könyvespolc **tetején** van.	**11** The plant is **on top of** the bookcase.
A dísztárgy **a** könyvespolc **felső részén** van.	**12** The ornament is **at the top of** the bookcase.
A tál **a** könyvespolc **közepén** van.	**13** The plate is **in the middle of** the bookcase.
A könyvek **a** könyvespolc **alján** vannak.	**14** The books are **at the bottom of** the bookcase.
A tányérok a könyvek **fölött** vannak.	**15** The plates are **above** the books.
A csészék a teáskancsó **alatt** vannak.	**16** The cups are **below** the teapot.
A teáskancsó a tál **mellett** van.	**17** The teapot is **beside/next to** the plate.
A tévé a képes folyóiratok **előtt** van.	**18** The television is **in front of** the magazines.
A képes folyóiratok a tévé **mögött** vannak.	**19** The magazines are **behind** the television.

The City 1 page 59

EST
GIVE WAY
130
REACH FOR A BETTER STANDARD
1
2
3
4
5
6
7
8
9
10
11
12
13
14
15
16
17
18
19

AT A CINEMA NEAR YOU
20
21
22
23
24

közlekedési tábla **1** road sign
parkolótábla **2** parking notice (*US* parking sign)
postaláda **3** letter-box/pillar-box (*US* mailbox)
eszpresszó **4** café (*also* cafe)
rendőr **5** police officer
járda **6** pavement (*US* sidewalk)
csatornanyílás-fedő **7** manhole cover
kanális **8** gutter
járdaszegély **9** kerb (*US* curb)
utca **10** street
utcasarok **11** street corner
bolt/üzlet **12** shop (*esp US* store)
forgalom **13** traffic
szemétgyűjtő **14** litter-bin (*US* trash can/garbage can)
újságos-stand **15** news-stand
újság **16** newspaper
újságárus **17** news-vendor (*Brit only*)
áruház **18** department store
zászló **19** flag

reklám/plakát **20** advertisement
szélfogó **21** bus shelter
buszmegálló **22** bus stop
gyár **23** factory
gyalogátkelő(hely) **24** pedestrian crossing (*US* crosswalk)

page 60

The City 2

1
2
3
4
5
6
7
8
9
10
QUEEN ANNE'S GATE

11
12
13
14
15
16
17
18

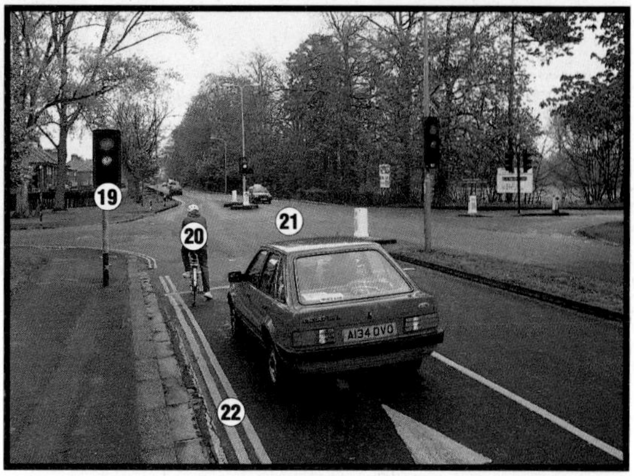
19
20
21
22
A134 DVO

23
24
25
26
MORREL

épület	**1**	building
park	**2**	park
babakocsi	**3**	pram (*US* baby carriage)
összecsukható gyerekkocsi	**4**	pushchair (*US* stroller)
mellékutca	**5**	side street
taxi	**6**	taxi/cab
lámpaoszlop	**7**	lamppost
gyalogos	**8**	pedestrian
kerítésrács	**9**	railings
utcanévtábla	**10**	street sign
hajó	**11**	boat
toronyház	**12**	tower block (*esp US* skyscraper)
ég(bolt)	**13**	sky
építészeti körvonal	**14**	skyline
híd	**15**	bridge
kirakodóhíd	**16**	pier
folyó	**17**	river
folyópart	**18**	bank
A peremvárosban		**In the suburbs**
közlekedési lámpák	**19**	traffic-lights (*US* traffic light)
kerékpáros	**20**	cyclist (*US* bicyclist)
útkereszteződés	**21**	crossroads (*US* intersection)
"megállni tilos" vonal	**22**	double yellow lines (*Brit only*)
útirányjelző tábla	**23**	signpost
autó/kocsi	**24**	car
emeletes autóbusz	**25**	double-decker bus
körforgalom	**26**	roundabout (*US* traffic circle/rotary)

Roads and Road Signs 1 page 61

1
GIVE WAY

2
STOP

13
14
15
16
17

3

4

18
19

5

6
30

7

8

9

10

11
Services ¼ m
P

12

elsőbbségadás kötelező	**1**	give way (*US* yield)
kötelező megállás	**2**	stop
behajtani tilos	**3**	no entry (*US* do not enter)
kétirányú forgalom	**4**	two-way traffic
megfordulni tilos	**5**	no U-turn
sebességkorlátozás	**6**	speed limit
balra kanyarodni tilos	**7**	no left turn
kettős kanyar jobbra	**8**	bend to right (*US* curve to right)
gyalogos és kerékpáros út(vonal)	**9**	cycle and pedestrian route (*US* bike and pedestrian path)
egyirányú utca	**10**	one-way street
pihenőhely/szolgáltatások	**11**	service station (*US* service area)
kötelező haladási irány (jobbra)	**12**	turn right
útépítés	**13**	roadworks (*US* road work)
dömper	**14**	dumper (truck) (*esp US* dump truck)
útépítő munkás	**15**	construction worker
légkalapács	**16**	pneumatic drill (*US also* jackhammer)
útjelző bója	**17**	cone
földgyalu/bulldózer	**18**	JCB (*US* backhoe)
talaj	**19**	soil

page 62

Roads and Road Signs 2

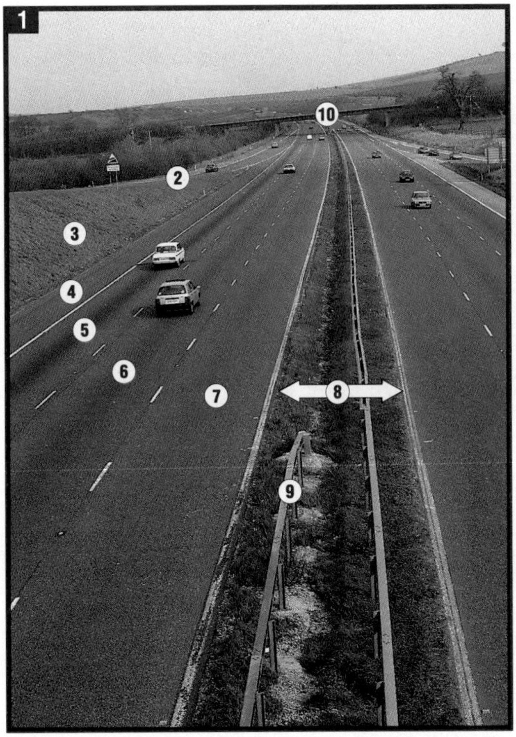
1
10
2
3
4
5
6
7
8
9

11
20
12
19
18
17
16
15
14
13

autópálya/sztráda **1** motorway (*Brit*)
felhajtó sáv **2** slip-road (*Brit*)
töltés **3** embankment (*Brit*)
útpadka **4** hard shoulder (*Brit*)
belső sáv/lassú sáv **5** inside lane/slow lane (*Brit*)
középső sáv **6** middle lane/centre lane (*Brit*)
külső sáv/gyors sáv **7** outside lane/fast lane (*Brit*)
elválasztó sáv **8** central reservation (*Brit*)
védőkorlát **9** crash barrier (*Brit*)
felüljáró (híd) **10** flyover (*Brit*)

autópálya/államok közti autópálya **11** freeway/ interstate highway (*US*)
lehajtó sáv **12** exit ramp (*US*)
töltés **13** bank (*US*)
útpadka **14** shoulder (*US*)
jobb(oldali) sáv/lassú sáv **15** right lane/slow lane (*US*)
középső sáv **16** center lane/middle lane (*US*)
bal(oldali) sáv/gyors sáv/előző sáv **17** left lane/fast lane/ passing lane (*US*)
elválasztó sáv **18** median strip (*US*)
védőkorlát **19** guardrail (*US*)
felüljáró (híd) **20** overpass (*US*)

21
22
25
23
24

aluljáró **21** underpass
gyalogos felüljáró **22** footbridge
pázsitszegély **23** grass verge (*US* shoulder)
országút/közút **24** road (*US* highway)
közúti elágazás **25** junction (*esp US* intersection)

Vehicles page 63

1

9

2
NATIONAL EXPRESS
Rapide
NATIONAL EXPRESS

10

11

3
Shell

12

13

4
MICHELIN
LEYLAND
MICHELIN
CHARLIE BROWNS

14

15

5

6

7

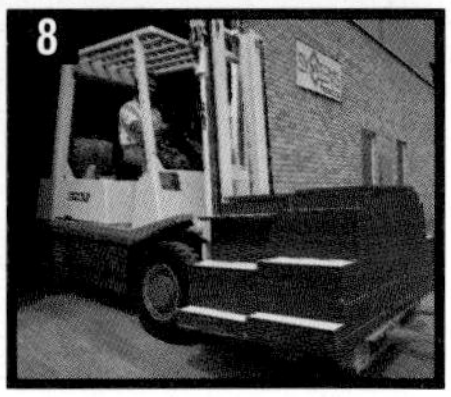
8

szállítójármű	**1**	transporter
autóbusz	**2**	coach (*US* bus)
tartálykocsi	**3**	tanker (*US* fuel truck)
teherautó	**4**	lorry (*US* truck)
furgon	**5**	van
cementkeverő autó	**6**	cement-mixer (*US* cement truck)
kis teherautó	**7**	pick-up truck
villás emelőtargonca	**8**	fork-lift truck
lakókocsi	**9**	caravan (*US* trailer)
dzsip	**10**	jeep
sportkocsi	**11**	sports car
szalonkocsi	**12**	saloon (*US* sedan)
kabriolet	**13**	convertible
kombi	**14**	estate (*US* station wagon)
kompakt/háromajtós kocsi	**15**	hatchback

page 64

The Car

benzinkút **1** filling-station (*US also* gas station)
visszapillantó tükör **2** wing mirror (*US* side mirror)
irányjelző/index **3** indicator (*US* turn signal)
fényszóró **4** headlight
rendszámtábla **5** number-plate (*US* license plate)
kipufogócső **6** exhaust-pipe
lökhárító **7** bumper
hátsó lámpa **8** rear-light (*US* taillight)
csomagtartó **9** boot (*US* trunk)
hátsó ablaktörlő **10** rear windscreen wiper (*US* rear windshield wiper)
benzintöltő pumpa **11** petrol pump (*US* gas pump)
gumitömlő **12** hose
töltőfej **13** nozzle
motorháztető **14** bonnet (*US* hood)
motor **15** engine
légszűrő **16** air filter
hengerfej **17** cylinder head
hűtőrács **18** radiator grille

szélvédő (üveg) **19** windscreen (*US* windshield)
műszerfal **20** dashboard
sebességváltó (kar) **21** gear lever (*US* gearshift)
volán/kormány **22** steering-wheel
üzemanyagmérő **23** fuel gauge (*US also* gas gauge)
sebességmérő **24** speedometer
gyújtás **25** ignition
kuplung **26** clutch
fékpedál **27** footbrake
gázpedál **28** accelerator (*US also* gas pedal)

Bikes page65

1
2
3
4
5
6
7
8
9
10
11
12
13
14
15
16

17
18
19
20

21
22
23
24

25
26
27
28
29

kerékpár/bicikli	**1**	bicycle/bike
nyereg	**2**	saddle (*esp US* seat)
pumpa	**3**	pump
váz	**4**	frame
hajtókar	**5**	crank
lakat	**6**	lock
küllők	**7**	spokes
lánc	**8**	chain
pedál	**9**	pedal
lánckerék	**10**	chain-wheel
szelep	**11**	valve
kerékagy	**12**	hub
sebességváltó (fogantyú)	**13**	gear lever (*US* gear changer)
macskaszem	**14**	reflector
huzal/kábel	**15**	cable
fék(fogantyú)	**16**	brake lever

háromkerekű bicikli	**17**	tricycle
csengő	**18**	bell
kormány	**19**	handlebar
kerék	**20**	wheel
robogó	**21**	scooter
sárhányó	**22**	mudguard (*US* fender)
ülés	**23**	seat
csomagtartó (doboz)	**24**	top box (*US* top case)
motorkerékpár	**25**	motor cycle (*Brit also* motor bike)
gáz(markolat)	**26**	accelerator/throttle
gumiabroncs	**27**	tyre (*US* tire)
motor	**28**	engine
lengéscsillapító	**29**	shock absorbers

page 66

The Railway (*US* Railroad)

1
2
3
4

← WAY OUT
5
6
7
8
9

10
All stations
11
12
13
14
15
16

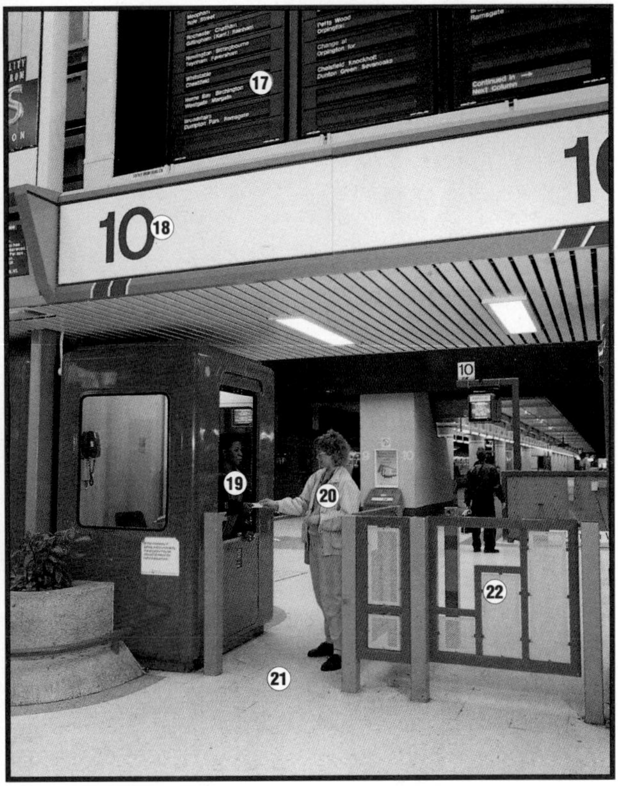
17
10
18
19
20
21
22

vasúti őrház **1** signal-box (*US* signal tower)
vasúti átjáró **2** level crossing (*US* grade crossing)
mozdony **3** engine
vasúti kocsi **4** coach (*US* passenger car)

A Metró **The Underground (*US* The Subway)**
'kijárat' tábla **5** exit sign
platform **6** platform
vágány(ok) **7** line(s) (*esp US* track)
metrószerelvény **8** train
alagút **9** tunnel

A vasútállomáson **At the Station**
jegypénztár **10** ticket office (*US* ticket counter)
ablak **11** window
sor **12** queue (*US* line)
táska **13** bag
bőrönd **14** suitcase
menetrend **15** timetable
hátizsák **16** rucksack (*esp US* backpack)
'induló vonatok' tábla **17** departures board (*US* departure board)
vágányszám **18** platform number (*US* track number)
jegykezelő **19** ticket-collector (*US* ticket taker)
utas **20** passenger
bejárat (a 10-es vágányhoz) **21** entrance (to platform 10)
kapu **22** barrier (*esp US* gate)

At the Airport 1 page 67

1
All Hold Baggage is
2
3
4

5
Channel Islands
International passengers
6

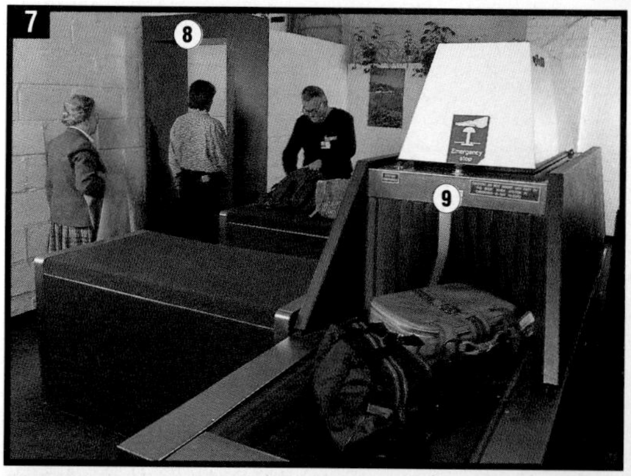
7
8
9

10
CAMERAS
BOURNEMOUTH INTERNATIONAL AIRPORT
JEWELLERY
PERFUMES
11

12
15
14
13

16
17
18

19
20

A terminálban	**In the terminal**
bejelentkezés	**1** check-in
repülőjegy	**2** airline ticket
beszállókártya	**3** boarding pass
bejelentkezési pult	**4** check-in desk (*US* check-in counter)
útlevélvizsgálat	**5** passport control
útlevél	**6** passport
biztonsági ellenőrzés	**7** security
fémdetektor (kapu)	**8** metal detector
csomagvizsgáló-röntgen	**9** X-ray scanner
vámmentes üzlet	**10** duty-free shop
parfüm	**11** perfume
indulási váró(csarnok)	**12** departures lounge (*US* departure lounge/ waiting area)
ülés	**13** seat
utaskísérő/stewardess	**14** steward (*US* flight attendant)
kapu	**15** gate
poggyászfelvétel	**16** luggage reclaim (*US* baggage reclaim)
poggyász	**17** luggage
poggyászkocsi	**18** trolley (*US* cart)
vám	**19** customs
vámőr	**20** customs officer

page 68

At the Airport 2

1
G-BGMO
2
3

4
5

6
7

8

9
10
11

12
AirUK
19
18
G-BGMO
JERSEY EUROPEAN
17
14
13
15
16

beszállás	**1**	boarding
utas	**2**	passenger
csomagszállító kocsi	**3**	trailer (*US* cart)
irányítótorony	**4**	control tower
légi(forgalom) irányító	**5**	air traffic controller
felszállás	**6**	take-off
kifutópálya	**7**	runway
leszállás	**8**	landing
helikopter	**9**	helicopter
légcsavar	**10**	rotor
pilóta	**11**	pilot
repülőgép	**12**	plane
orr(-rész)	**13**	nose
pilótafülke	**14**	cockpit
légcsavar	**15**	propeller
szárny	**16**	wing
repülőgéptörzs	**17**	fuselage
farok(rész)	**18**	tail
sugárhajtómű	**19**	jet engine

In Port 1 page 69

1
2
3
4
5
6
7
8

9
SALLY PUMPKIN
OXFORD

10
11
12
13

14
RX56
15
16
17

18

19
20

vitorláshajó **1** sailing-ship
árbóc **2** mast
vitorla **3** sail
fedélzet **4** deck
kabin **5** cabin
hajókötél **6** cable (*US* line)
evezőscsónak **7** rowing-boat (*US* rowboat)
evezőlapát **8** oar
bárka **9** barge

jachtkikötő **10** marina
motorcsónak **11** motor boat
jacht **12** yacht (*US also* sailboat)
lakóhajó **13** cabin cruiser
halászhajó **14** fishing boat
horgonyzás **15** mooring
orrtőke **16** bow
tat **17** stern
mentőhajó **18** lifeboat
kajak **19** canoe (*US* kayak)
kajak-evezőlapát **20** paddle

page 70

In Port 2

1
2
3
4
5

6

7

8

12
13
14
15

9
10
RED FUNNEL

11

16

dokk	**1**	dock
daru	**2**	crane
kikötői raktár	**3**	warehouse
hajórakomány	**4**	cargo
hajó	**5**	ship
tankhajó	**6**	(oil-)tanker
szárnyashajó	**7**	hydrofoil
légpárnás hajó	**8**	hovercraft
komp	**9**	ferry
hajókémény	**10**	funnel (*US* smokestack)
óceánjáró	**11**	liner (*esp US* ocean liner)
világítótorony	**12**	lighthouse
sziklák	**13**	rocks
felfújható gumicsónak	**14**	inflatable dinghy (*US* rubber raft)
csónakmotor/farmotor	**15**	outboard motor
horgony	**16**	anchor

Holidays 1 (*US* Vacations) page 71

1
2
3
4

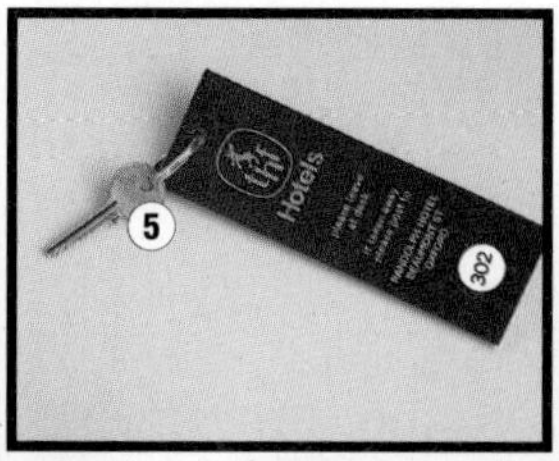
5
Hotels
302

6

7

8

9
10
11
12

13

14

15
16

17

18
19
20
21
22

23
24
25

26
27

hotelporta/recepció	**1** hotel reception (*US* front desk)
londiner/szállodai hordár	**2** porter (*US also* bellhop)
vendég	**3** guest
hotelportás	**4** receptionist
szobakulcs	**5** room key
egyágyas szoba	**6** single room
franciaágyas szoba	**7** double room
kétágyas szoba	**8** twin room (*US* room with twin beds)
városnézés	**9** sightseeing
idegenvezető	**10** tour guide
turistacsoport	**11** party of tourists
turista	**12** tourist
vár	**13** castle
kastély/udvarház	**14** country house
falu	**15** village
vidék	**16** the countryside
(társas) kirándulás	**17** picnic
kempingezés	**18** camping
sátor	**19** tent
sátorfenék	**20** groundsheet
hálózsák	**21** sleeping-bag
kempingfőző	**22** camping stove (*US* camp stove)
(gyalog)túrázás	**23** hiking
túrázó	**24** hiker
hátizsák	**25** rucksack (*esp US* backpack)
lakókocsi-tábor	**26** caravan site (*US* trailer camp)
lakókocsi	**27** caravan (*US* trailer)

page 72

Holidays 2 (*US* Vacations)

1
2
3
4
5

6
7
8
9

10

11
12

13
14
15

16

17

18
19

20
21

22
23

24
25
26

a tengerpart	**1**	the seaside (*esp US* the beach)
üdülőhely	**2**	holiday resort
tengerpart/strand	**3**	beach
védőgát	**4**	sea wall
sétány	**5**	promenade (*esp US* seafront)
tengeri körutazás	**6**	cruise
napozóágy/nyugágy	**7**	sunbed
napfürdőző	**8**	sunbather
napernyő	**9**	sunshade
vitorlázás	**10**	sailing
üdülés hajón	**11**	boating holiday (*US* boating vacation)
csatorna	**12**	canal
horgászás	**13**	fishing
horgász	**14**	angler
horgászbot	**15**	fishing-rod
lovaglás	**16**	pony-trekking (*US* horseback riding)
szafári	**17**	safari
ejtőernyőzés	**18**	parachuting
ejtőernyő	**19**	parachute
léghajózás	**20**	ballooning
hőlégballon	**21**	hot-air balloon
sárkányrepülés	**22**	hang-gliding
sárkányrepülő	**23**	hang-glider
hegymászás	**24**	climbing
hegymászó	**25**	climber
biztosító kötél	**26**	harness

The Environment page 73

1
2
3
4
5

6
7

8
9
10
11

12
13
14

15
16
17
18

19
20
21
22
23
24

25
26
27

28
29
30

hegy(ség)	**1**	mountain
(hegy)csúcs	**2**	peak
völgy	**3**	valley
tó	**4**	lake
erdő(ség)	**5**	forest
vízesés	**6**	waterfall
patak	**7**	stream
tenger	**8**	sea
sziklák	**9**	rocks
tengerpart/strand	**10**	beach
(szikla)szirt	**11**	cliff
(kis) hegy	**12**	hill
víztároló	**13**	reservoir
völgyzárógát	**14**	dam
sivatag	**15**	desert
homok	**16**	sand
homokdűne	**17**	sand-dune
fennsík	**18**	plateau
erdő	**19**	wood (*esp US* woods)
tanya/farm	**20**	farm
gazdasági lakóépület	**21**	farmhouse
szérű/pajta	**22**	barn
(mesterséges) tó	**23**	pond
mező	**24**	field
kombájn	**25**	combine harvester (*US* combine)
búzatábla	**26**	cornfield
(gabona)mag	**27**	grain
traktor	**28**	tractor
eke	**29**	plough (*esp US* plow)
barázda	**30**	furrow

page 74

Hobbies

1

2

3

4
5

6
7
8

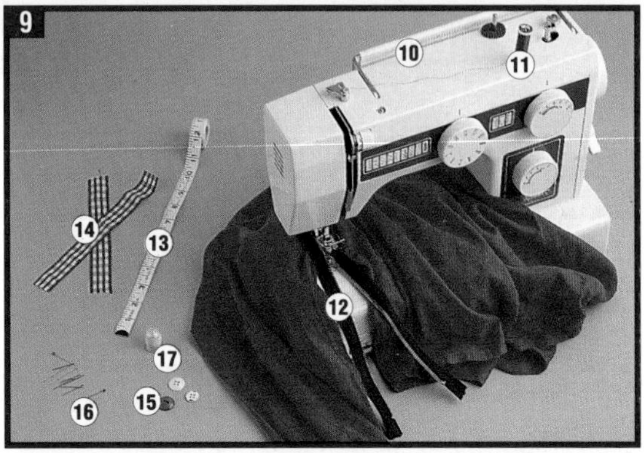
9
10
11
12
13
14
15
16
17

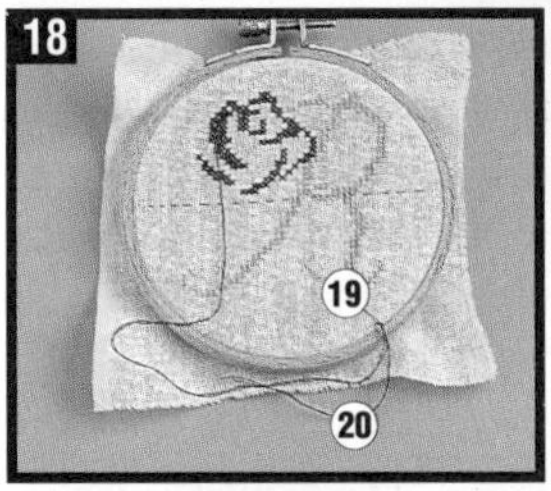
18
19
20

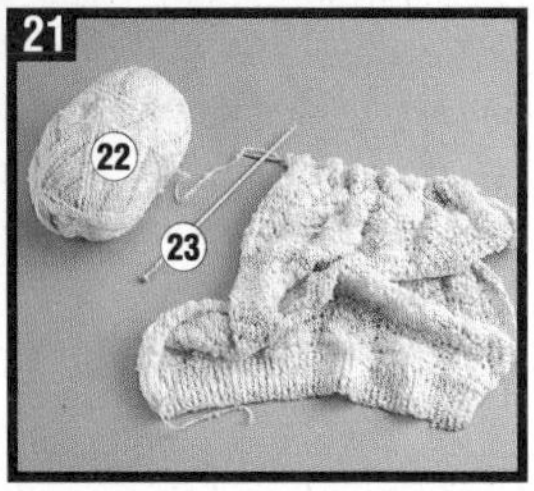
21
22
23

24
25
26
27
28
29
30
31
32
33
34

festés	**1** painting
rajzolás	**2** drawing
kerámiázás	**3** pottery
bélyeggyűjtés	**4** stamp collecting
bélyegalbum	**5** stamp album
modellezés	**6** making models
készlet	**7** kit
modell	**8** model
szabás-varrás	**9** sewing
varrógép	**10** sewing-machine
(egy) spulni cérna	**11** reel of cotton (*US* spool of thread)
cipzár	**12** zip (*esp US* zipper)
mérőszalag	**13** tape-measure
szalag	**14** ribbon
gomb	**15** button
gombostű	**16** pin
gyűszű	**17** thimble
hímzés	**18** embroidery
(varró)tű	**19** needle
fonal	**20** thread
kötés	**21** knitting
gyapjú(fonal)	**22** wool
kötőtű	**23** knitting-needle
ostábla (játék)	**24** backgammon
tábla	**25** board
dámajáték	**26** draughts (*US* checkers)
rázópohár	**27** shaker
dobókocka	**28** dice
sakk	**29** chess
(egy) pakli kártya	**30** pack of playing-cards
treff bubi	**31** jack/knave of clubs
kőr dáma	**32** queen of hearts
káró király	**33** king of diamonds
pikk ász	**34** ace of spades

Musical Instruments

page 75

1
2
3
4
5

6
7
8
9

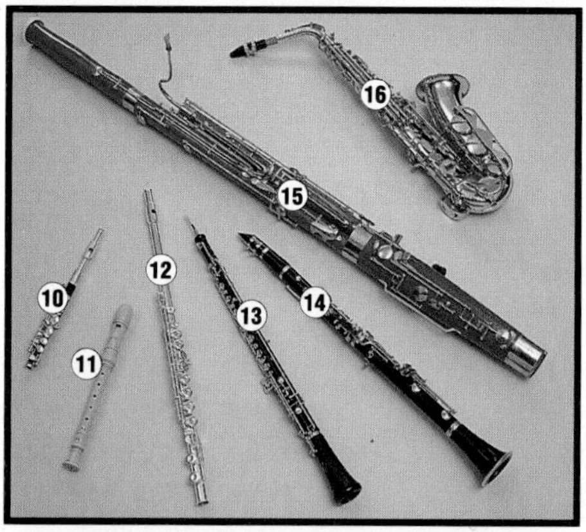
10
11
12
13
14
15
16

17
18
19
20
21
22

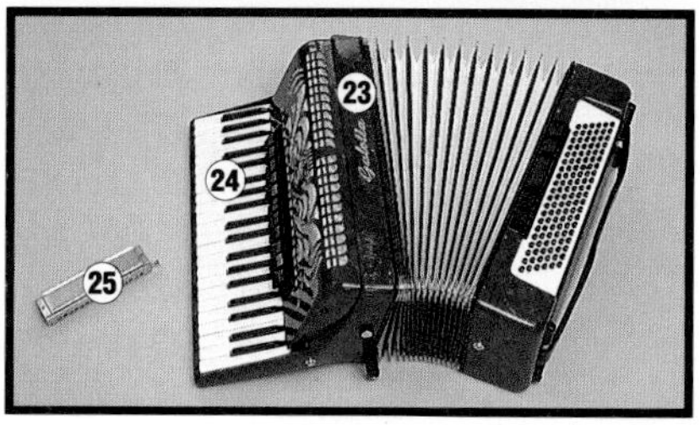
23
24
25

Vonós hangszerek	**Strings**
brácsa	**1** viola
vonó	**2** bow
cselló	**3** cello
hegedű	**4** violin
nagybőgő	**5** (double-)bass
Rézfúvós hangszerek	**Brass**
vadászkürt	**6** French horn
trombita	**7** trumpet
harsona	**8** trombone
tuba	**9** tuba
Fafúvós hangszerek	**Woodwind**
kisfuvola	**10** piccolo
furulya	**11** recorder
fuvola	**12** flute
oboa	**13** oboe
klarinét	**14** clarinet
fagott	**15** bassoon
szaxofon	**16** saxophone
Ütőhangszerek	**Percussion**
üstdob	**17** kettledrum
csörgődob	**18** tambourine
dobverők	**19** drumsticks
bongó	**20** bongos
cintányérok	**21** cymbals
konga	**22** conga
Egyéb hangszerek	**Other instruments**
tangóharmonika	**23** accordion
billentyűk	**24** keys
szájharmonika	**25** harmonica

page 76

Music and Theatre (*US* Theater)

1
2
3
4
5
6

23
24
25
26
27
28

7
8
9
10
11
12
13

14
15
16
17
18
19
20
21
22

Zene	**Music**
zenekar	**1** orchestra
zenész	**2** musician
zongora	**3** piano
karmester	**4** conductor
karmesterpálca	**5** baton
kotta	**6** sheet music
popegyüttes	**7** pop group
(elektromos) gitár	**8** (electric) guitar
énekes/szólista	**9** singer/vocalist
dob	**10** drum
dobos	**11** drummer
billentyűs	**12** keyboard player
szintetizátor	**13** synthesizer
A színház	**The Theatre (*US* Theater)**
díszlet	**14** scenery
színpad	**15** stage
színész	**16** actor
színésznő	**17** actress
színfalak	**18** wings
zenekari árok	**19** orchestra pit
földszinti ülések	**20** stalls (*US* orchestra seats)
erkélypáholy	**21** circle/balcony (*US* mezzanine)
karzat/kakasülés	**22** gallery (*US* balcony)
A filmszínház/mozi	**The Cinema (*US* Movie Theater)**
(film)vászon	**23** screen
filmsztár	**24** film star (*US* movie star)
jegyszedő	**25** usher
jegyszedőnő	**26** usher (*Brit also* usherette)
ülőhelyek közti átjáró	**27** aisle
közönség	**28** audience

Sports 1 page 77

1
2
3
4
5

6
7
8
9

10
11
12

13
14
15
16
17

18
19
20

21
22

23
24

25
26
27
28
29
30

(jég)korcsolyázás **1** ice-skating
korcsolyázik **2** skate (*verb*)
korcsolyázó **3** skater
jégkorcsolya **4** ice-skate
műjégpálya **5** ice-rink (*esp US* rink)
síelés **6** skiing
síel **7** ski (*verb*)
síbot **8** pole
síléc **9** ski
vízisíelés **10** water-skiing
vízisíel **11** water-ski (*verb*)
vízisíelő **12** water-skier
hullámlovaglás **13** surfing
hullám **14** wave
hullámlovagol **15** surf (*verb*)
hullámlovas **16** surfer
szörfdeszka **17** surfboard
széllovaglás/szörfözés **18** windsurfing
széllovas/szörfös **19** windsurfer
szörfdeszka **20** sailboard
oxigénpalackos könnyűbúvár-merülés **21** scuba-diving
oxigénpalack **22** (air)tank
légzőcsöves könnyűbúvár-merülés **23** snorkelling (*US* snorkeling)
légzőcső **24** snorkel
úszás **25** swimming
úszik **26** swim (*verb*)
úszó **27** swimmer
úszómedence **28** swimming-pool
fejest ugrik **29** dive (*verb*)
fejesugró/(mű)ugró **30** diver

page 78

Sports 2

1
2
3
4
5
6
7

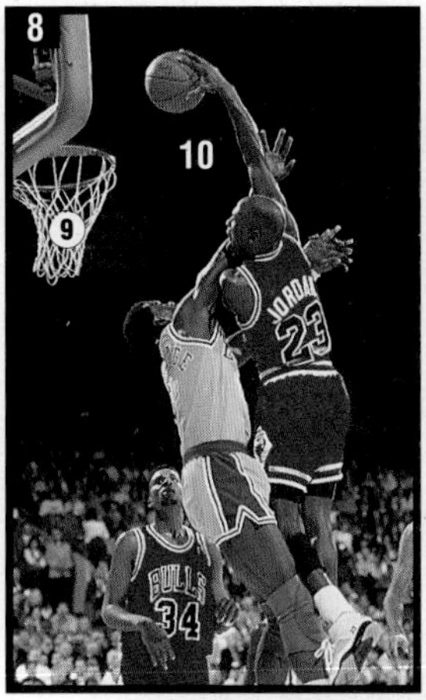
8
9
10

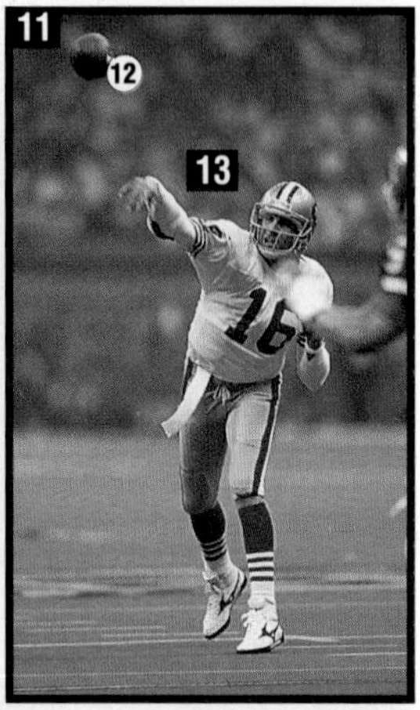
11
12
13

14
15

16
17
18
19

20
21

22
23

24
25

26
27
28

baseball	**1** baseball
baseball-sisak	**2** batting helmet
ütőjátékos	**3** batter
baseball-kesztyű	**4** baseball glove/mitt
fogóálarc	**5** face mask/catcher's mask
fogó(játékos)	**6** catcher
tömeg/közönség	**7** crowd
kosárlabda	**8** basketball
háló	**9** net
(kosárra) dob	**10** shoot (*verb*)
amerikai futball	**11** American football (*US* football)
futball	**12** football
dob/hajít	**13** throw (*verb*)
rögbi	**14** rugby
szerel	**15** tackle (*verb*)
gyeplabda/hoki	**16** hockey (*US* field hockey)
hokijátékos	**17** hockey player
hokibot	**18** hockey stick
hokilabda	**19** hockey ball
röplabda	**20** volleyball
ugrik	**21** jump (*verb*)
squash	**22** squash
(tenisz)ütő	**23** racket (*also* racquet)
tollaslabda (játék)	**24** badminton
tollaslabda	**25** shuttlecock
asztalitenisz/pingpong	**26** table tennis (*esp US* ping-pong)
pingpongütő	**27** table tennis bat (*US* paddle)
üt	**28** hit (*verb*)

Sports 3 page 79

1
2
3

4
5
6
7

17
20
22
18
20
21
19

23
25
24

8
10
9

11
12
SUTTON
14
15
16
13

26
27

28
29

célbadobó játék(nyíl)	**1** darts
céltábla (nyíljátéké)	**2** dartboard
céloz	**3** aim (*verb*)
amerikai biliárd	**4** snooker
biliárddákó	**5** cue
biliárdasztal	**6** table
golyótartó	**7** pocket
tekézés	**8** bowling
tekepálya	**9** bowling-alley
tekebábuk	**10** pins
golf	**11** golf
labdaszedő és ütőhordó	**12** caddy
játéktér	**13** fairway
célterület	**14** green
golfütő	**15** club
lyuk	**16** hole
bokszolás	**17** boxing
sarok	**18** corner
ring/szorító	**19** ring
kötelek	**20** ropes
bokszkesztyű	**21** boxing glove
ökölcsapás/ütés	**22** punch (*verb*)
birkózás	**23** wrestling
birkózik	**24** wrestle (*verb*)
játékvezető	**25** referee
dzsúdó	**26** judo
rúg	**27** kick (*verb*)
karate	**28** karate
csap/vág	**29** chop (*verb*)

page 80

Sports 4

GOLD SEAL OAKS

torna	**1** gymnastics
tornász	**2** gymnast
kerékpározás	**3** cycling
kerékpározik	**4** cycle (*verb*)
autóversenyzés	**5** motor-racing (*US* auto racing)
autóversenypálya	**6** racetrack
versenyautó	**7** racing car (*US* race car)
autóversenyző	**8** racing driver (*US* race car driver)
lovaglás	**9** riding (*US* horseback riding)
lovagol	**10** ride (*verb*)
lovas	**11** rider
nyereg	**12** saddle
kengyel(vas)	**13** stirrups
gyeplő	**14** reins
atlétika	**15** athletics (*US* track and field)
ugró-és dobóterület	**16** field
futópálya	**17** track
nézők	**18** spectators
(futó)sáv	**19** lane
atléta	**20** athlete
fut	**21** run (*verb*)
rajtgép	**22** starting-block
lóversenyzés	**23** horse-racing
versenylovagol	**24** race (*verb*)
versenyló	**25** racehorse
zsoké	**26** jockey
indító-box	**27** starting-gate
lóversenypálya	**28** racecourse (*esp US* racetrack)

Sports 5 page 81

1
2
3
4
5
6
6
7

8
9
10
11

12
13
14
15
16
17
18
19
20
21
22

23
24
25
26
27
28
29
30

Tenisz	**Tennis**
egyéni mérkőzés	**1** singles match
adogat	**2** serve (*verb*)
adogató	**3** server
alapvonal	**4** baseline
adogatóvonal	**5** service line
oldalvonalak	**6** tramlines (*US* sidelines)
háló	**7** net
páros mérkőzés	**8** doubles match
labdaszedő (fiú)	**9** ballboy
teniszpálya	**10** tennis-court
vezetőbíró	**11** umpire

Krikett	**Cricket**
krikettmérkőzés	**12** cricket match
krikettkapus	**13** wicket-keeper
ütőjátékos	**14** batsman
láb(szár)védő	**15** pads
dobóterület	**16** pitch
labdavető	**17** bowler
labdát vet	**18** bowl (*verb*)
krikettkapu	**19** wicket/stumps
játékvezető	**20** umpire
mezőnyjátékos	**21** fielder
mezőny/pálya	**22** field
Futball	**Football (*esp US* Soccer)**
góllövés	**23** scoring a goal
lelátó	**24** stand
partjelző	**25** linesman
gólt rúg	**26** score (*verb*)
kapufa	**27** goalpost
gól	**28** goal
elhibáz/mellélő	**29** miss (*verb*)
kapus	**30** goalkeeper

page 82

Keeping Fit (*US* Keeping in Shape)

3
1
2

15
16
26
24
27
25
19
23
18
17
22
20
21

4
5
6
8
7

14
13
12
9
11
10

gyalogol/sétál	**1**	walk (*verb*)
kocog	**2**	jog (*verb*)
kocogó	**3**	jogger
ugróasztalozás	**4**	trampolining
(le)esik	**5**	fall (*verb*)
ugróasztal	**6**	trampoline
edző/oktató	**7**	instructor
visszapattan/felugrik	**8**	bounce (*verb*)
dob	**9**	throw (*verb*)
elkap	**10**	catch (*verb*)
hintázik	**11**	swing (*verb*)
(mászó)kötél	**12**	rope
felmászik/kapaszkodik	**13**	climb (*verb*)
bordásfal	**14**	wall bars
tornaterem	**15**	gym/gymnasium
átugrik (valamit)	**16**	vault (*verb*)
(torna)szőnyeg	**17**	mat
ugrószekrény	**18**	vaulting-horse
nyújtóz(kod)ik	**19**	stretch (*verb*)
hátrahajol	**20**	bend over backwards (*verb*) (*US* bend over backward)
térdel	**21**	kneel (*verb*)
előrehajol	**22**	bend over (*verb*)
sípol	**23**	blow a whistle (*verb*)
síp	**24**	whistle
kézenáll	**25**	do a handstand (*verb*)
ugrálókötél	**26**	skipping-rope (*US* jump rope)
ugrálókötelezik/szökdel	**27**	skip (*verb*)

Verbs 1 page 83

1

2

3

4

Vasal/Inget **vasal**.	**1** He is **ironing**/He's **ironing** a shirt.
Főz/Ételt **főz**.	**2** He is **cooking**/He's **cooking** a meal.
Tisztít/Ablakot **tisztít**.	**3** He is **cleaning**/He's **cleaning** a window.
Varr.	**4** He is **sewing**.

5

6

7

8

Söpör/A járdát **söpri**.	**5** He is **sweeping**/He's **sweeping** the path (*US also* walk).
Beköt egy zsákot/Zsákot **köt be**.	**6** He is **tying up** a bag/He's **tying** a bag **up**.
Ás/**Ássa** a talajt.	**7** He is **digging**/He's **digging** the soil.
Felteker egy tömlőt/Tömlőt **teker fel**.	**8** He is **winding up** a hose/He's **winding** a hose **up**.

9

10

11

12

Megtölti az elektromos vízforralót.	**9** She is **filling** a kettle (*US* an electric teakettle).
A víz **forr**.	**10** The water is **boiling**.
Beleönti a vizet a teáskancsóba.	**11** She is **pouring** the water into a teapot.
Keveri a teáját.	**12** She is **stirring** her tea.

page 84

Verbs 2

13
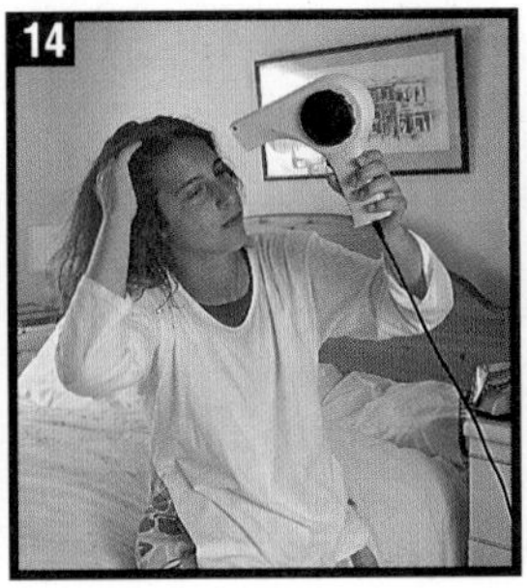
14

15

16

Mossa a haját. **13** She is **washing** her hair.
Szárítja a haját. **14** She is **drying** her hair.
Fésüli a haját. **15** She is **combing** her hair.
Keféli a haját. **16** She is **brushing** her hair.

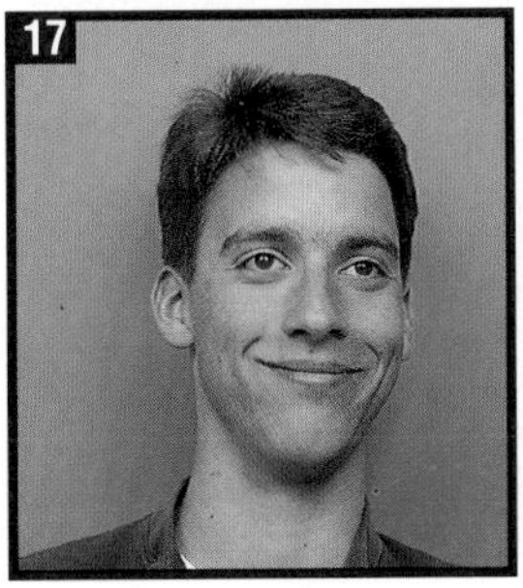
17
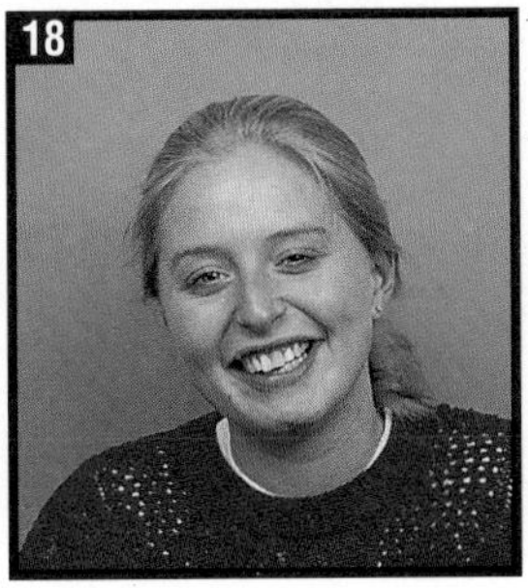
18
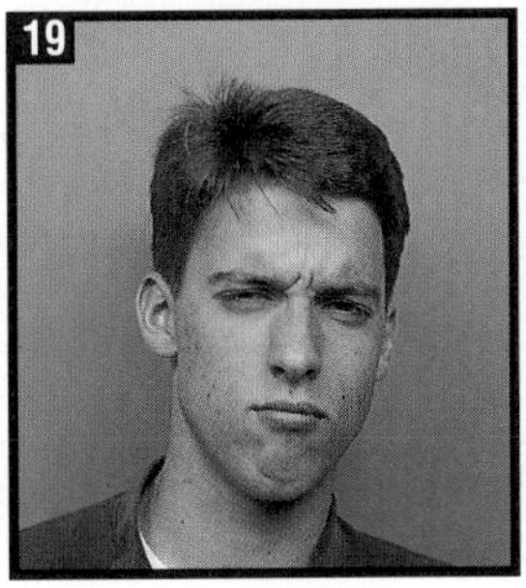
19
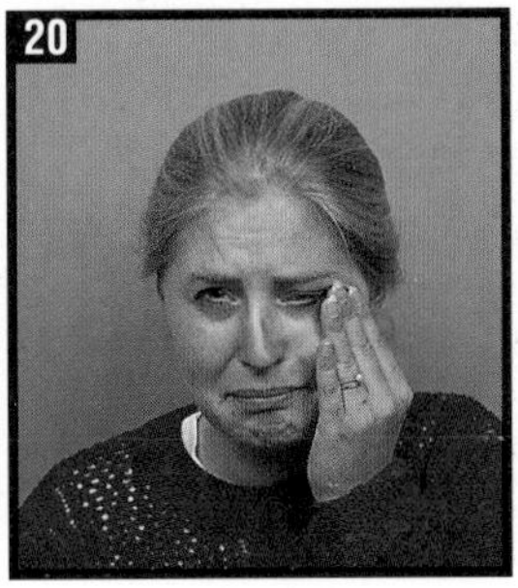
20

Mosolyog. **17** He is **smiling**.
Nevet. **18** She is **laughing**.
Összehúzza a szemöldökét/Rosszallóan néz. **19** He is **frowning**.
Sír. **20** She is **crying**.

21

22

23

24

Ül. **21** He is **sitting**.
Áll. **22** He is **standing**.
Fekszik. **23** He is **lying down**.
Alszik. **24** He is **sleeping**.

Verbs 3 page 85

1

2

3

4

Kezet fognak.	**1** They are **shaking** hands.
Megcsókolja a gyereket.	**2** She is **kissing** the child.
Megöleli a gyereket.	**3** She is **hugging** the child.
Integet a gyereknek.	**4** She is **waving** to the child.

5

6

7

8

Beszél hozzá/**Beszélget** vele.	**5** She is **speaking** to him/She is **talking** to him.
Énekelnek.	**6** They are **singing**.
Táncolnak.	**7** They are **dancing**.
Tapsolnak.	**8** They are **clapping**.

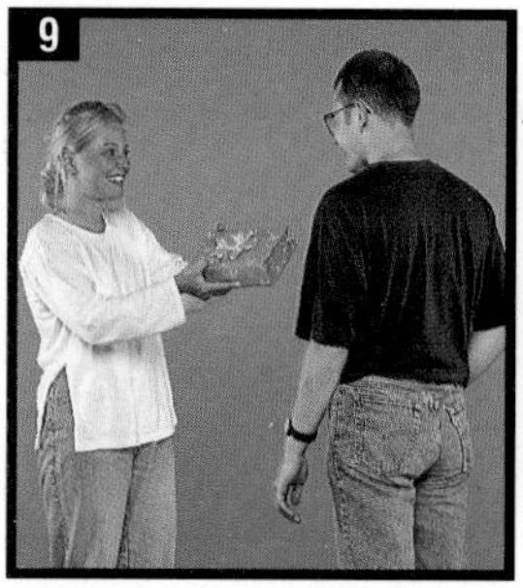
9
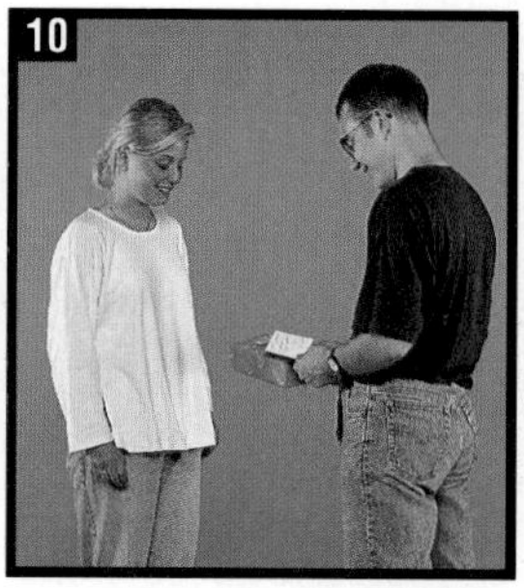
10

11

12

Ajándékot **ad** neki.	**9** She is **giving** him a present.
Átveszi az ajándékot tőle.	**10** He is **taking** the present from her.
Kibontja az ajándékot.	**11** He is **opening** the present.
Olvassa a könyvet.	**12** He is **reading** the book.

page 86

Verbs 4

13

14

15

16

Felemeli a bőröndöt. **13** She is **lifting** the suitcase.
Viszi a bőröndöt. **14** She is **carrying** the suitcase.
Tartja a bőröndöt. **15** She is **holding** the suitcase.
Leteszi a bőröndöt. **16** She is **putting** the suitcase **down**.

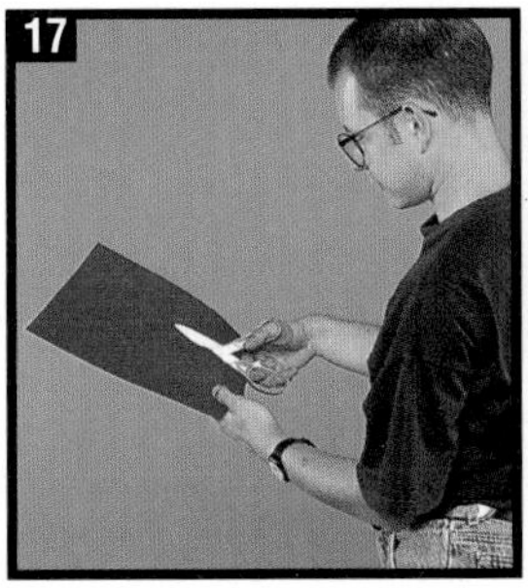
17

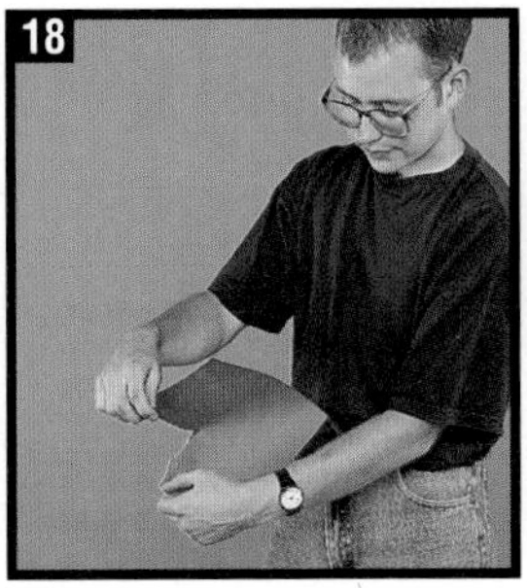
18

19

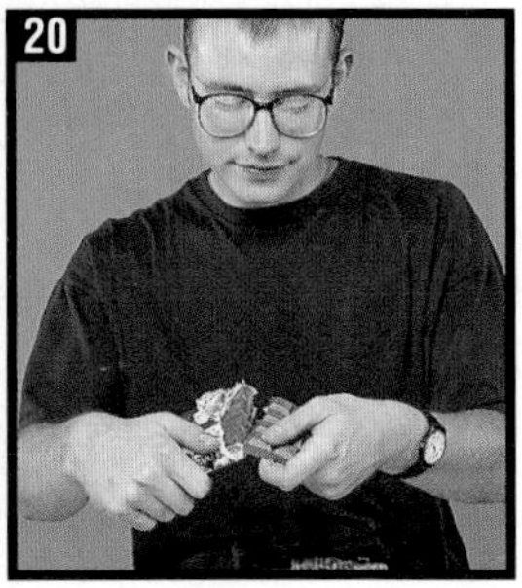
20

Elvág egy (darab) papírt. **17** He is **cutting** a piece of paper.
Eltép egy (darab) papírt. **18** He is **tearing** a piece of paper.
Összehajt egy (darab) papírt. **19** He is **folding** a piece of paper.
Eltör egy tábla csokoládét. **20** He is **breaking** a bar of chocolate.

21

22

23

24

Tol egy kiskocsit. **21** She is **pushing** a trolley (*US* cart).
Húz egy kiskocsit. **22** She is **pulling** a trolley (*US* cart).
Meggyújt egy gyertyát. **23** He is **lighting** a candle.
A gyertya **ég**. **24** The candle is **burning**.

Contrastive Adjectives 1 page 87

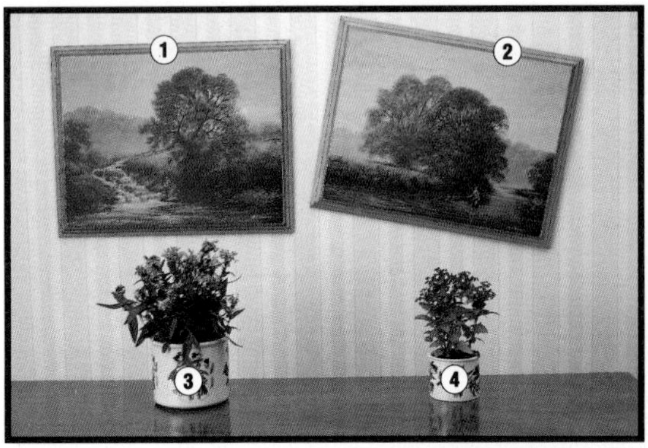
1
2
3
4

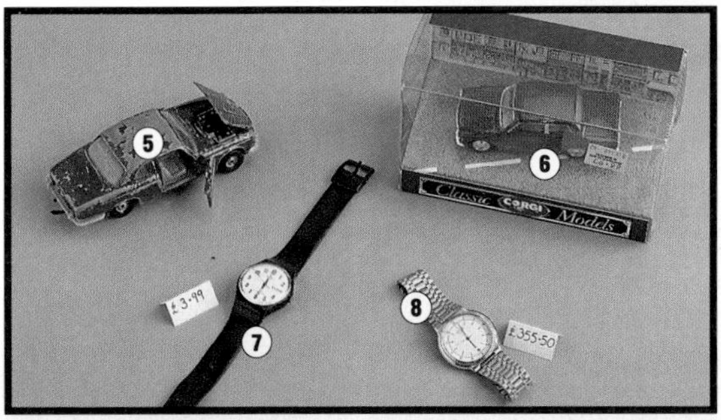
5
6
Classic CORGI Models
£3-99
7
8
£355-50

9
OXFORD ADVANCED LEARNER'S DICTIONARY
NEW EDITION
10
$2 + 2 = 4$
11
$f(x) = \frac{1}{(x - 4)(x + 2)}$
12

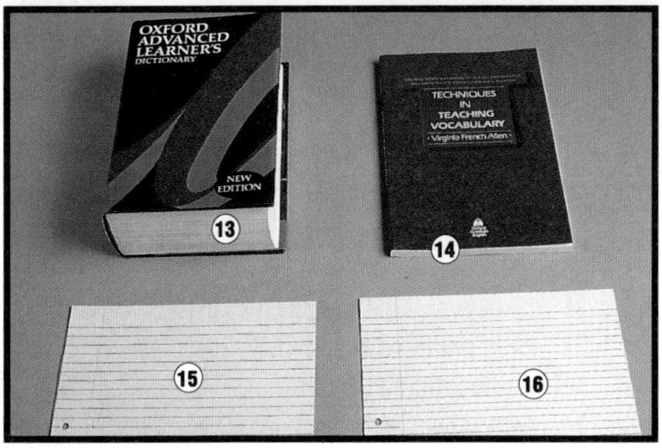
OXFORD ADVANCED LEARNER'S DICTIONARY
NEW EDITION
13
TECHNIQUES IN TEACHING VOCABULARY
Virginia French Allen
14
15
16

17

18

19

20

21

22

23
4

24

egyenes	**1**	straight
ferde	**2**	crooked
nagy/terjedelmes	**3**	big/large
kicsi/apró	**4**	little/small
régi	**5**	old
új	**6**	new
olcsó	**7**	cheap
drága	**8**	expensive
nyitott	**9**	open
csukott	**10**	closed
egyszerű	**11**	easy
bonyolult	**12**	difficult
vastag	**13**	thick
vékony	**14**	thin
széles	**15**	wide
keskeny	**16**	narrow
magas	**17**	high
alacsony	**18**	low
mély	**19**	deep
sekély	**20**	shallow
gyenge	**21**	weak
erős	**22**	strong
gyors	**23**	fast
lassú	**24**	slow

page 88

Contrastive Adjectives 2

1

2

3

4

5

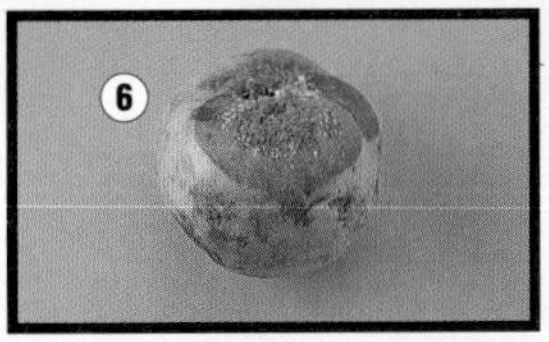
6

7

8

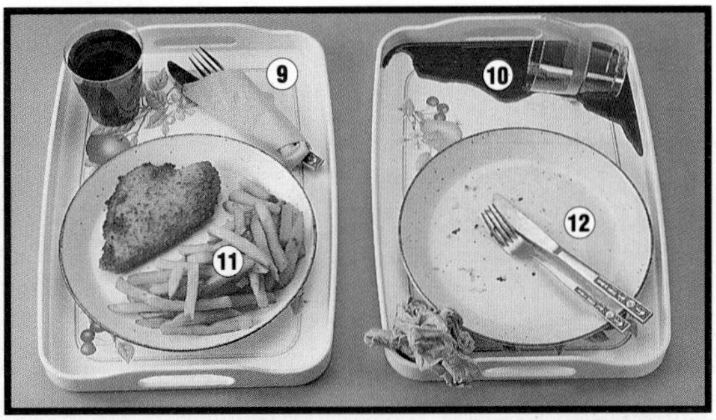
9
10
11
12

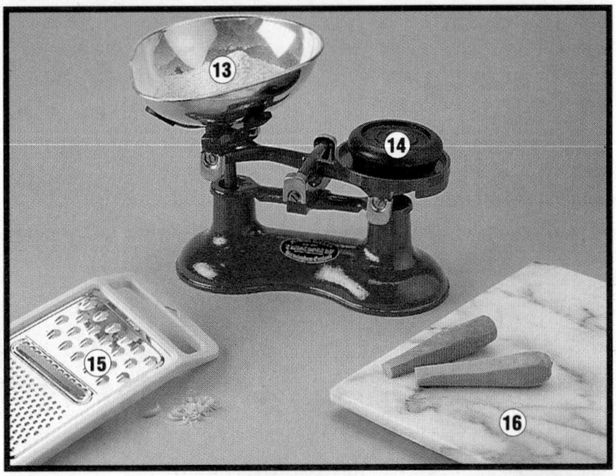
13
14
15
16

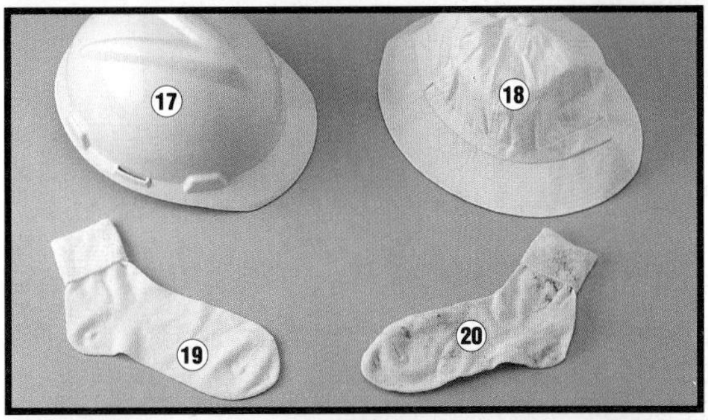
17
18
19
20

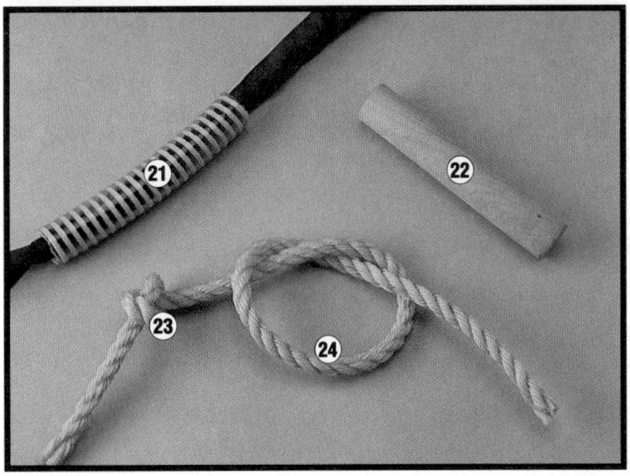
21
22
23
24

boldog/vidám	**1**	happy
szomorú/boldogtalan	**2**	sad/unhappy
hangos	**3**	loud
csendes	**4**	quiet
jó	**5**	good
rossz	**6**	bad
rendes	**7**	tidy (*esp US* neat)
rendetlen	**8**	untidy (*esp US* messy)
száraz	**9**	dry
nedves	**10**	wet
tele	**11**	full
üres	**12**	empty
könnyű	**13**	light
nehéz/súlyos	**14**	heavy
érdes/durva	**15**	rough
sima	**16**	smooth
kemény	**17**	hard
puha	**18**	soft
tiszta	**19**	clean
piszkos	**20**	dirty
üreges	**21**	hollow
tömör	**22**	solid
szoros	**23**	tight
laza	**24**	loose

Animals 1 page 89

1
2

3

4

5

6

7

8

9
10

11
12

13
14

15
16
17

tehén	**1**	cow
borjú	**2**	calf
bika	**3**	bull
denevér	**4**	bat
sün(disznó)	**5**	hedgehog
mókus	**6**	squirrel
róka	**7**	fox
kecske	**8**	goat
juh	**9**	sheep
bárány	**10**	lamb
szamár	**11**	donkey
pata	**12**	hoof
ló	**13**	horse
csikó	**14**	foal
póni(ló)	**15**	pony
sörény	**16**	mane
farok	**17**	tail

Pets Háziállatok

18
19
20
21

22
23
24

25

26

macska	**18**	cat
(macska)bajusz	**19**	whiskers
bunda/szőr	**20**	fur
kismacska/cica	**21**	kitten
kutya	**22**	dog
kiskutya/kölyökkutya	**23**	puppy
mancs	**24**	paw
hörcsög	**25**	hamster
nyúl	**26**	rabbit

Animals 2

page 90

szarvas	**1**	deer
agancs	**2**	antler
farkas	**3**	wolf
medve	**4**	bear
karom	**5**	claw
jegesmedve	**6**	polar bear
panda	**7**	panda
kenguru	**8**	kangaroo
erszény	**9**	pouch
teve	**10**	camel
púp	**11**	hump
láma	**12**	llama
majom	**13**	monkey
gorilla	**14**	gorilla
zebra	**15**	zebra
oroszlán	**16**	lion
tigris	**17**	tiger
leopárd	**18**	leopard
bivaly	**19**	buffalo
szarv	**20**	horn
rinocérosz	**21**	rhinoceros
víziló	**22**	hippopotamus
zsiráf	**23**	giraffe
elefánt	**24**	elephant
agyar	**25**	tusk
ormány	**26**	trunk
fóka	**27**	seal
uszony	**28**	flipper
delfin	**29**	dolphin
bálna	**30**	whale

1
2

3

4
5

6

7

8
9

10
11

12

13

14

15

16

17

18

19
20

21

22

23

24
25
26

29

27
28

30

Fish and Reptiles page 91

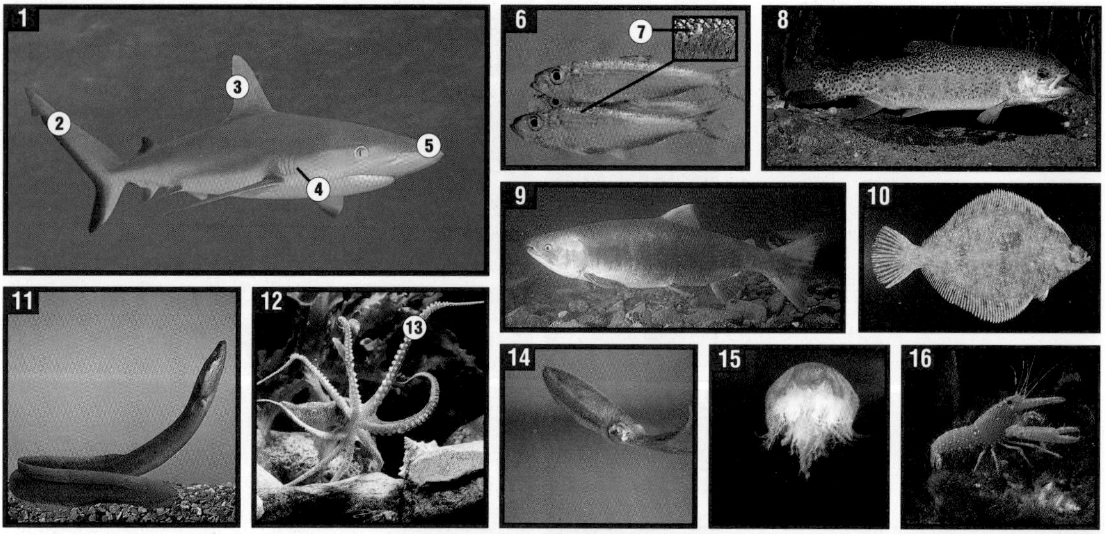

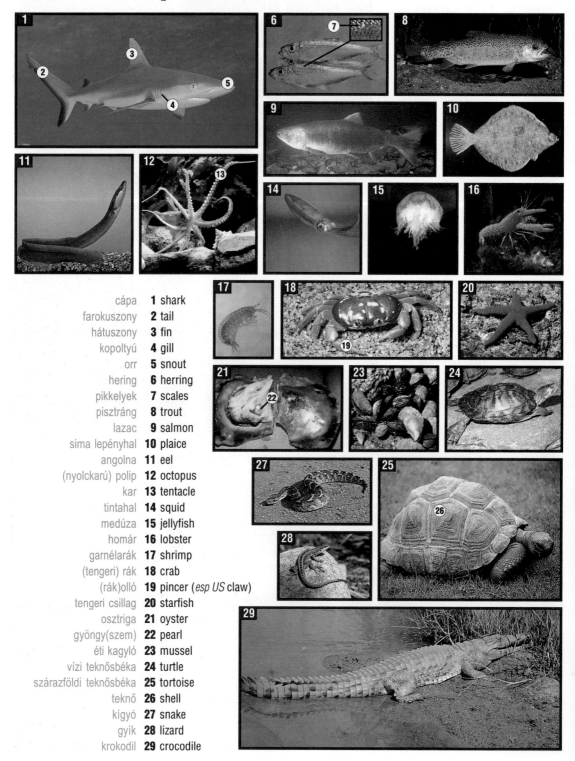

cápa **1** shark
farokuszony **2** tail
hátuszony **3** fin
kopoltyú **4** gill
orr **5** snout
hering **6** herring
pikkelyek **7** scales
pisztráng **8** trout
lazac **9** salmon
sima lepényhal **10** plaice
angolna **11** eel
(nyolckarú) polip **12** octopus
kar **13** tentacle
tintahal **14** squid
medúza **15** jellyfish
homár **16** lobster
garnélarák **17** shrimp
(tengeri) rák **18** crab
(rák)olló **19** pincer (*esp US* claw)
tengeri csillag **20** starfish
osztriga **21** oyster
gyöngy(szem) **22** pearl
éti kagyló **23** mussel
vízi teknősbéka **24** turtle
szárazföldi teknősbéka **25** tortoise
teknő **26** shell
kígyó **27** snake
gyík **28** lizard
krokodil **29** crocodile

page 92

Insects and Other Animals

1

2
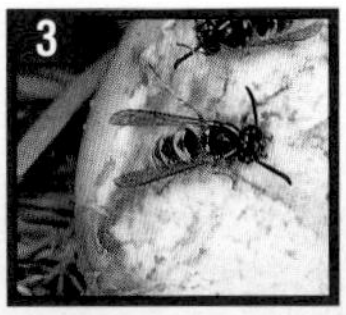
3

4

5

6
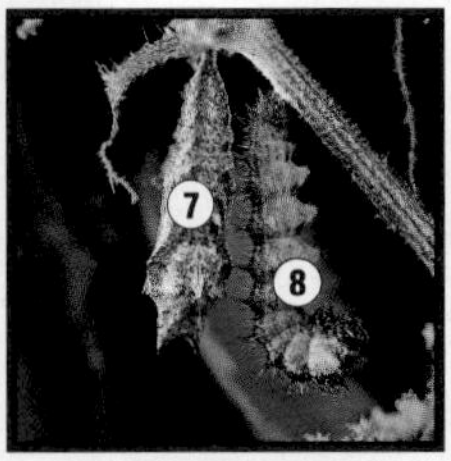
7
8

9
10
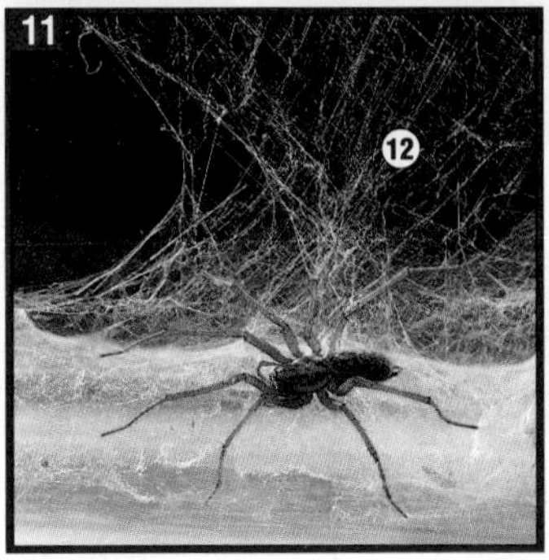
11
12

13
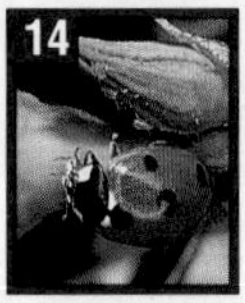
14

15

16

17

18

19
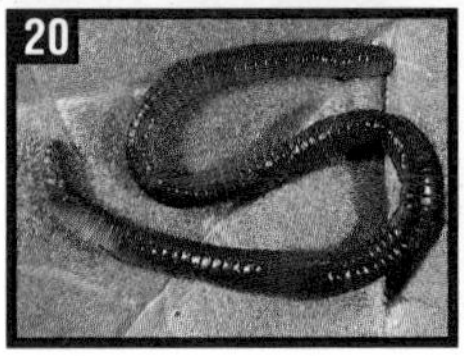
20
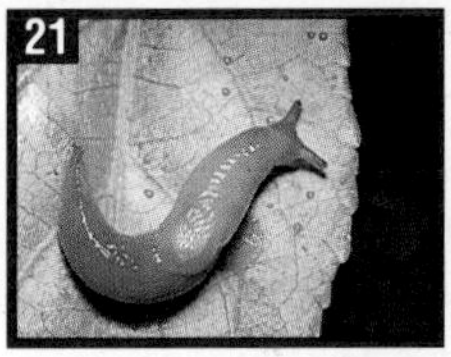
21

22

23
24

25

légy **1** fly
méh **2** bee
darázs **3** wasp
szúnyog **4** mosquito
szitakötő **5** dragonfly
pillangó **6** butterfly
selyem(hernyó)gubó **7** cocoon
hernyó **8** caterpillar
(moly)lepke **9** moth
tapogatócsáp **10** antenna
pók **11** spider
pókháló **12** (cob)web
bogár **13** beetle
katicabogár **14** ladybird (*US* ladybug)
hangya **15** ant
svábbogár **16** cockroach (*also* roach)
szöcske **17** grasshopper
tücsök **18** cricket
ájtatos manó **19** praying mantis
giliszta **20** worm
meztelen csiga **21** slug
csiga **22** snail
skorpió **23** scorpion
fullánk **24** sting
béka **25** frog

Birds page 93

1
2
3
4
5

6
7

8
9

10
11
12
13
14
15

16
17
18
19
20
21
22
23
24
25
26
27
28
29
30
31

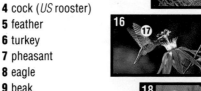

csirke	**1** chicken
tyúk	**2** hen
csibe	**3** chick
kakas	**4** cock (*US* rooster)
(madár)toll	**5** feather
pulyka	**6** turkey
fácán	**7** pheasant
sas	**8** eagle
csőr (ragadozó madáré)	**9** beak
sólyom	**10** hawk
varjú	**11** crow
bagoly	**12** owl
fészek	**13** nest
galamb	**14** pigeon
veréb	**15** sparrow
kolibri	**16** hummingbird
szárny	**17** wing
kanári	**18** canary
papagáj	**19** parrot
törpepapagáj	**20** budgerigar (*US* parakeet)
fecske	**21** swallow
strucc	**22** ostrich
pingvin	**23** penguin
páva	**24** peacock
flamingó	**25** flamingo
csőr (vízimadáré)	**26** bill
liba/lúd	**27** goose
kacsa	**28** duck
úszóhártyás láb	**29** webbed foot
(tengeri) sirály	**30** (sea)gull
hattyú	**31** swan

Foneticus jelek/Brit és amerikai jelölések

Magánhangzók és kettőshangzók

1	iː	mint a	**see** / siː /	szóban	11	ɜː	mint a	**fur** / fɜː(r) /	szóban
2	ɪ	mint a	**sit** / sɪt /	szóban	12	ə	mint az	**ago** / ə'gəʊ /	szóban
3	e	mint a	**ten** / ten /	szóban	13	eɪ	mint a	**page** / peɪdʒ /	szóban
4	æ	mint a	**hat** / hæt /	szóban	14	əʊ	mint a	**home** / həʊm /	szóban
5	ɑː	mint az	**arm** / ɑːm /	szóban	15	aɪ	mint a	**five** / faɪv /	szóban
6	ɒ	mint a	**got** / gɒt /	szóban	16	aʊ	mint a	**now** / naʊ /	szóban
7	ɔː	mint a	**saw** / sɔː /	szóban	17	ɔɪ	mint a	**join** / dʒɔɪn /	szóban
8	ʊ	mint a	**put** / pʊt /	szóban	18	ɪə	mint a	**near** / nɪə(r) /	szóban
9	uː	mint a	**too** / tuː /	szóban	19	eə	mint a	**hair** / heə(r) /	szóban
10	ʌ	mint a	**cup** / kʌp /	szóban	20	ʊə	mint a	**pure** / pjʊə(r) /	szóban

Mássalhangzók

1	p	mint a	**pen** / pen /	szóban	13	s	mint a	**so** / səʊ /	szóban
2	b	mint a	**bad** / bæd /	szóban	14	z	mint a	**zoo** / zuː /	szóban
3	t	mint a	**tea** / tiː /	szóban	15	ʃ	mint a	**she** / ʃiː /	szóban
4	d	mint a	**did** / dɪd /	szóban	16	ʒ	mint a	**vision** / 'vɪʒn /	szóban
5	k	mint a	**cat** / kæt /	szóban	17	h	mint a	**how** / haʊ /	szóban
6	g	mint a	**got** / gɒt /	szóban	18	m	mint a	**man** / mæn /	szóban
7	tʃ	mint a	**chin** / tʃɪn /	szóban	19	n	mint a	**no** / nəʊ /	szóban
8	dʒ	mint a	**June** / dʒuːn /	szóban	20	ŋ	mint a	**sing** / sɪŋ /	szóban
9	f	mint a	**fall** / fɔːl /	szóban	21	l	mint a	**leg** / leg /	szóban
10	v	mint a	**voice** / vɔɪs /	szóban	22	r	mint a	**red** / red /	szóban
11	θ	mint a	**thin** / θɪn /	szóban	23	j	mint a	**yes** / jes /	szóban
12	ð	mint a	**then** / ðen /	szóban	24	w	mint a	**wet** / wet /	szóban

/ ' / jelöli a főhangsúlyt pl. **about** / ə'baʊt /
/ ˌ / jelöli a mellékhangsúlyt pl. **academic** / ˌækə'demɪk /

(r) A zárójelben lévő ‘r’ a brit angol kiejtésben akkor hallható, ha közvetlenül utána magánhangzó áll. Egyéb esetekben a kiejtésben néma marad.
Az amerikai angol kiejtésben mind a fonetikus átírású, mind a normál helyesírású ‘r’-t ejtjük.

A brit és amerikai angol jelölések szerepe

Brit motorway (*Brit*)
jelöli, hogy egy szó csak a brit angolban használatos

US zip code (*US*)
jelöli, hogy egy szó csak az amerikai angolban használatos

jug (*US* pitcher)
jelöli, hogy a (jug) szó, amely csak a brit angolban használatos, ugyanazt jelenti, mint a (pitcher) szó, de az utóbbi csak az amerikai angolban fordul elő

Brit also red (*Brit also* ginger)
jelöli, hogy a (red) szó, amely a brit és az amerikai angolban egyaránt használatos, ugyanazt jelenti, mint a (ginger) szó, de az utóbbi csak a brit angolban fordul elő

US also blackboard (*US also* chalkboard)
jelöli, hogy a (blackboard) szó, amely a brit és az amerikai angolban egyaránt használatos, ugyanazt jelenti, mint a (chalkboard) szó, amely csak az amerikai angolban fordul elő

esp US sofa (*esp US* couch)
jelöli, hogy az elsősorban a brit angolban használt, de az amerikai angolban is előforduló (sofa) szó ugyanazt jelenti, mint a (couch) szó, de az utóbbi az amerikai angolban gyakoribb

Index

Index page 101

Index

Betűrendes mutató

Betűrendes mutató

People and Health Pages 1-8

1 Who's who?

Read the sentences about this family and then write the names in the family tree.

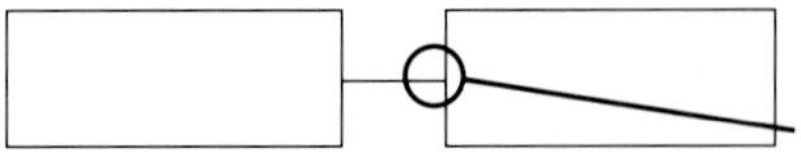
= is married to

Peter is married to Ann and they have a daughter called Laura.
Peter's parents are Jack and Rosy.
Ann's sister, Sarah, has a son called Leo.

Linda is Ann's sister-in-law.
Alan's mother-in-law is called Joan.
Jamie is Leo's cousin.
Bill has got two grandsons and one granddaughter.

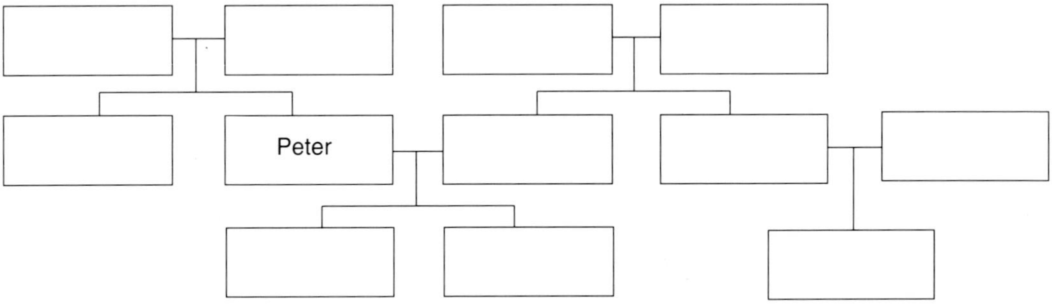
Peter

2 The Human Body

There are sixteen parts of the body hidden in this square. Can you find them all?

thumb

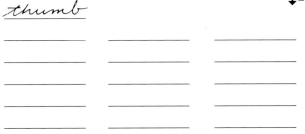

e	i	b	h	e	a	d	e	n	o	x
o	y	u	e	a	m	o	o	a	t	s
t	o	e	o	u	b	i	f	i	s	t
a	e	z	o	m	e	f	i	l	o	o
n	c	a	u	e	c	a	n	g	e	m
k	e	h	i	e	a	h	g	i	i	a
l	t	e	i	o	u	e	e	i	o	c
e	e	a	o	n	a	i	r	s	e	h
u	l	u	o	e	t	x	u	e	t	e
a	i	b	a	c	k	a	e	e	i	e
e	p	a	i	k	n	e	e	t	e	k

3 What's the matter?

Match what the patient says to the doctor's advice.

Patient

a I have dreadful earache.
b I've got a sore throat and a temperature.
c I've fallen over and hurt my arm.
d I've got a small scratch on my leg.
e I've got terrible toothache.

a 3 b ___ c ___ d ___ e ___

Doctor

1 Take two of these tablets and go straight to bed.
2 You probably need a filling.
3 Put two drops in each ear twice a day.
4 We'll need to put it in a sling.
5 Put some of this ointment on it and then cover it with a plaster.

Exercises page 127

Clothes Pages 9-12

1 Test your memory!

Look carefully at page 10.

Fill in the missing words in the sentences below. Use words from the box.

a The woman is wearing a ________________ blouse and a ________________ blue jacket.

b The boy is wearing a ________________ blazer and ________________ trousers.

c The man is wearing a red and white ________________ tie and he is carrying a raincoat.

d The girl is wearing a ________________ coat and a ________________ scarf.

polka-dot tartan pink grey striped plain patterned

■ *Language note*

The man in the picture is **wearing** a suit and he is **carrying** a raincoat.

2 What other things are people carrying in the picture? Write some sentences.

____

____

____

____

____

3 Match each of these words with the right part of the body.

trainer	head
belt	hand
watch	neck
glove	waist
tights	foot
helmet	legs
tie	wrist

4 Find the words from the mixed-up letters. They are all things that people wear or carry. When you have finished, read down the box to find the mystery word.

1 FRIEHCEKHDAN
2 FRASC
3 LABRUMEL
4 ERUPS
5 RECIFEABS
6 RENGIRA
7 LACKENCE
8 NABAHGD
9 GIRN
10 LOSECAHE
11 LAWLET
12 GESSNALUSS

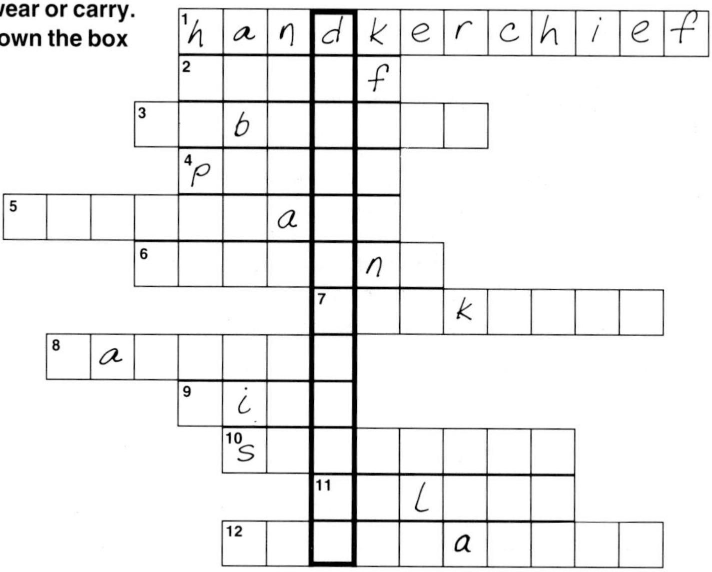
handkerchief

At Home Pages 15-22 and 58

1 Find the word in each group that is different from the others.

a mug cup freezer saucer teapot

b scales aftershave soap shampoo toothpaste

c wardrobe sideboard vase wall unit chest of drawers

d duster brush scourer oven mop

e rake watering-can shears lawnmower bush

2 Write in the words.

a ____________

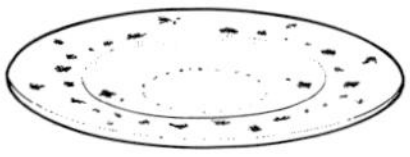

b ____________

c ____________

d ____________

e ____________

f ____________

g ____________

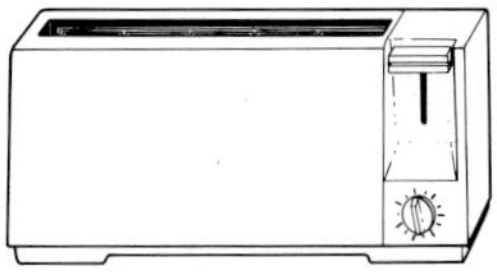

h ____________

3 Test your memory!

Look at page 18 for two minutes, then read these sentences about the picture. Decide if they are true or false.

a The box of tissues is in the bedside cabinet.
b There's a poster over the bed.
c There's a hair-drier on the dressing table.
d The dressing table is in front of the chest of drawers.
e The blanket is under the bedspread.
f There's a coat-hanger betweeen the light and the alarm clock.

If the sentences are false, write them correctly.

Exercises page 129

Shopping and Food Pages 23-28

1 Match a word in A with the right word in B.

A	B
a tube of	chocolate
a loaf of	cereal
a bar of	toothpaste
a bottle of	margarine
a jar of	jam
a packet of	bread
a tub of	biscuits
a box of	mineral water

2 Complete these dialogues using words from the box. Use each word only once.

1 a Can I help you?
  b Yes, please. How much are the ____________________?
  a They're 70p a bunch.
  b And the strawberries?
  a 85p a ____________________.

2 a I'd like some ____________________ for my wife's birthday.
  b Certainly, sir. Any particular kind?
  a Well, yes, she likes these blue ones.
  b Oh, you mean ____________________.

3 a I'm looking for a ____________________ of chocolates. Have you got any?
  b They're up on the top ____________________.
  a They're a present for somebody so I'll need a roll of ____________________ and a ____________________ of Sellotape too, please.

4 a Are you ready to order? Here comes the ____________________.
  b No, I haven't decided yet. Are you going to have a ____________________?
  a Yes, I think I'll have the melon.

flowers	bananas	starter	shelf	punnet	waiter	wrapping paper	irises	box	reel

3 Where do each of the conversations in exercise 2 take place?

1 ____________________ 3 ____________________

2 ____________________ 4 ____________________

Dates and Times Pages 33 and 37

1 Look at the clocks, then find two ways of saying each time, using the expressions in the box.

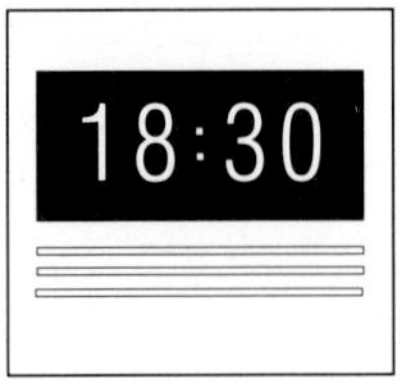
18:30

1 c, ______ 2 ______

00:00

3 ______ 4 ______

14:45

5 ______ 6 ______

- a midnight
- b ten to five
- c eleven fifty-five
- d four fifty
- e a quarter to three in the afternoon
- f six thirty pm
- g seven minutes past four
- h two forty-five pm
- i half past six in the evening
- j twelve o'clock at night
- k five to twelve
- l four o seven

2 Dates

John always forgets important dates so he writes them down at the beginning of the year in a special page in his diary.

Look at the page, then answer the questions by writing the dates **in words**.

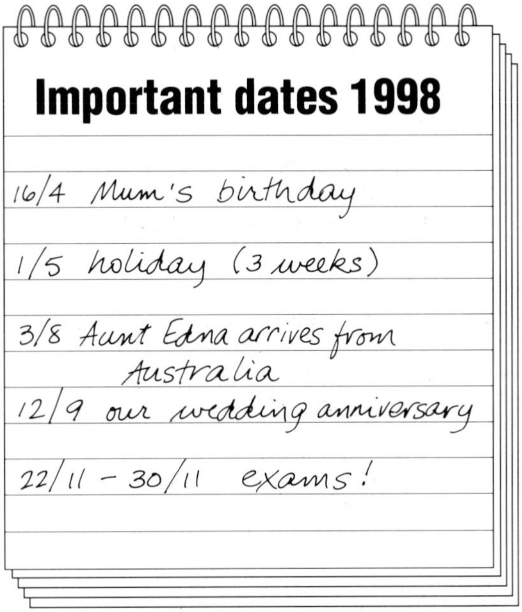
Important dates 1998
16/4 Mum's birthday
1/5 holiday (3 weeks)
3/8 Aunt Edna arrives from Australia
12/9 our wedding anniversary
22/11 – 30/11 exams!

a When is John's mother's birthday?

______

b When does John's holiday begin?

______

c On what date does Aunt Edna arrive?

______

d When is John's wedding anniversary?

______

e On what date do his exams finish?

______

Exercises page 131

At Work Pages 39-40 and 43-44

1 What do we call someone who...

...reads the news aloud on the radio or TV?

...arranges people's holidays for them?

...works with wood?

... makes bread and cakes?

...treats sick animals?

...repairs cars?

2 Read these job advertisements and decide what job is being offered in each one.

a Ladies' and gentlemen's ***** needed for modern salon. Experience of cutting all types of hair necessary.

b ***** for long-distance deliveries. Must have licence.

c WANTED! Qualified ***** for small chemist's. Duties to include dispensing prescriptions plus general shop work.

d EXPERIENCE IN RADIO? Love all kinds of music? 'Joy FM' is looking for a *****.

a

b

c

d

3 Office wordsearch

There are thirteen words connected with the office in this square. Can you find them all?

e	a	n	d	i	s	k	a	i	l	s
i	o	c	h	e	q	u	e	o	e	i
u	b	o	i	e	s	y	f	u	t	w
f	c	t	t	a	i	k	d	n	t	a
t	i	e	y	u	n	r	i	g	e	a
e	u	l	p	e	e	r	a	c	r	i
i	e	i	e	l	p	u	r	d	x	x
n	g	r	p	i	u	o	y	a	e	u
e	c	a	o	o	i	e	f	m	i	o
s	t	e	o	x	p	u	u	o	y	e
s	n	o	t	e	b	o	o	k	a	e

cheque

Describing Things Pages 47-49 and 87-88

1 Write the names of these shapes.

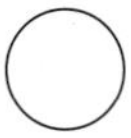

a ____________ b ____________

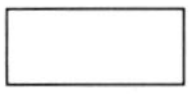

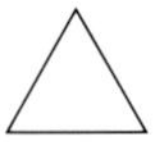

c ____________ d ____________

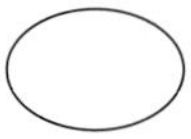

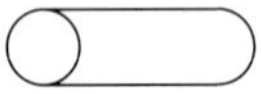

e ____________ f ____________

■ *Language note*

We say: This page is **rectangular**.
(Not: **a rectangle.**)
Rectangular is an adjective.

Noun	*Adjective*
rectangle	rectangular
triangle	triangular
circle	circular
oval	oval
square	square
cylinder	cylindrical

2 Match these questions and answers by writing the correct number next to the questions.

Question		*Answer*
a What shape is it?		1 It's used for measuring things and for drawing straight lines.
b How much does it weigh?		2 This one is made of plastic but they are also made of wood.
c How big is it?		3 It's rectangular.
d What's it made of?		4 About 10g.
e What's it used for?		5 It's about 15 cm long, 3 cm wide and 0.2 cm thick.

What is it? It's on page 49 of this dictionary. ____________

3 Find the opposites of these adjectives and write them in the puzzle.

1 crooked
2 thin
3 light
4 tight
5 empty
6 hollow
7 dry

Now read down the box to find another adjective!

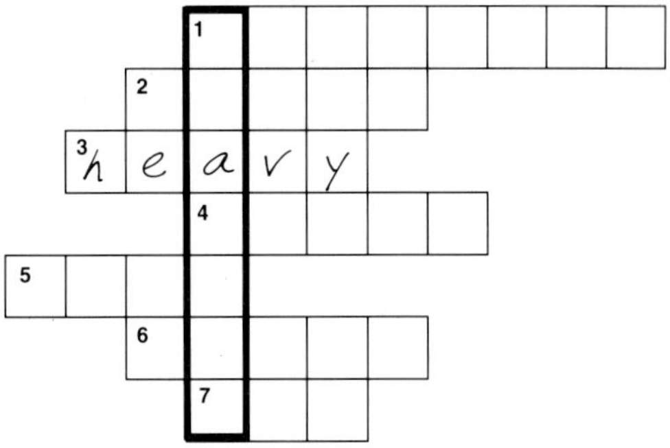
1
2
3 h e a v y
4
5
6
7

Exercises page 133

The Weather Pages 51-52 and 56

1 Look at the weather map of the British Isles below. Find a symbol for each of the words in the box and draw it.

sun	cloud	rain
wind	fog	snow

■ *Language note*

The adjective from { **cloud** is **cloudy**. / **sun** is **sunny**. }

Make adjectives from the other words in the box. (If you are not sure about the spelling, check on page 51.)

wind ____________________

snow ____________________

fog ____________________

rain ____________________

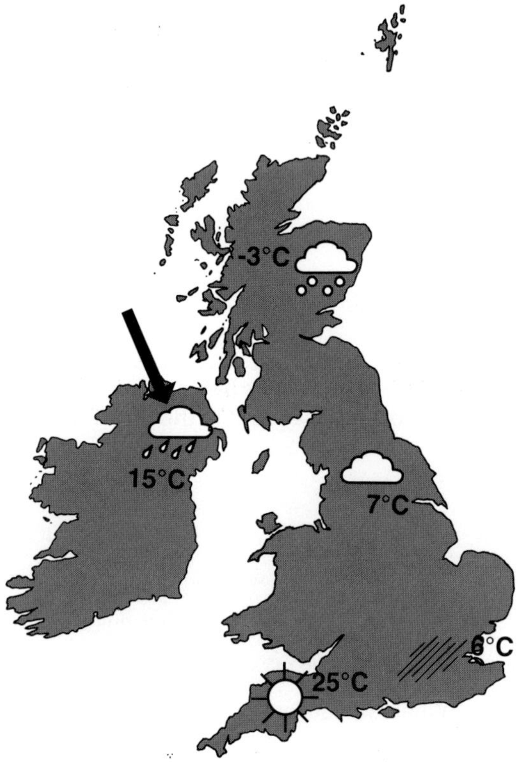
-3°C
15°C
7°C
6°C
25°C

2 Look at the weather map and write in the missing information below.

Tomorrow's Weather

The South-East will start the day quite (1) ____________________ and (2) ____________________, but in the South-West it's going to be rather (3) ____________________ and (4) ____________________. Further north it will be (5) ____________________ all day with a maximum (6) ____________________ of 7°C.

Over in Northern Ireland it will be (7) ____________________ with some (8) ____________________ during the morning and it will be very (9) ____________________ on the coast. Up in Scotland the temperature will fall to (10) ____________________ 3°C and there may be some (11) ____________________.

The City Pages 57 and 59-60

1 Letter-box or mailbox?

These are six things that you can find in a city street. Complete the table by writing the British or American words.

British	*American*
letter-box	
	sidewalk
crossroads	
	traffic circle
	trash can
pedestrian crossing	

2 Look at the pictures and complete the sentences using words from the box.

a

b

c

d

e

bus stop building pavement across away from
into road sign towards along road

a She is walking ______________________
the ______________________ .

b He is going ______________________ the
______________________ .

c She is going ______________________ the
______________________ .

d They are walking ______________________
the ______________________ .

e He is running ______________________
the ______________________ .

Exercises page 135

Travelling Pages 63-68

1 Label these pictures.

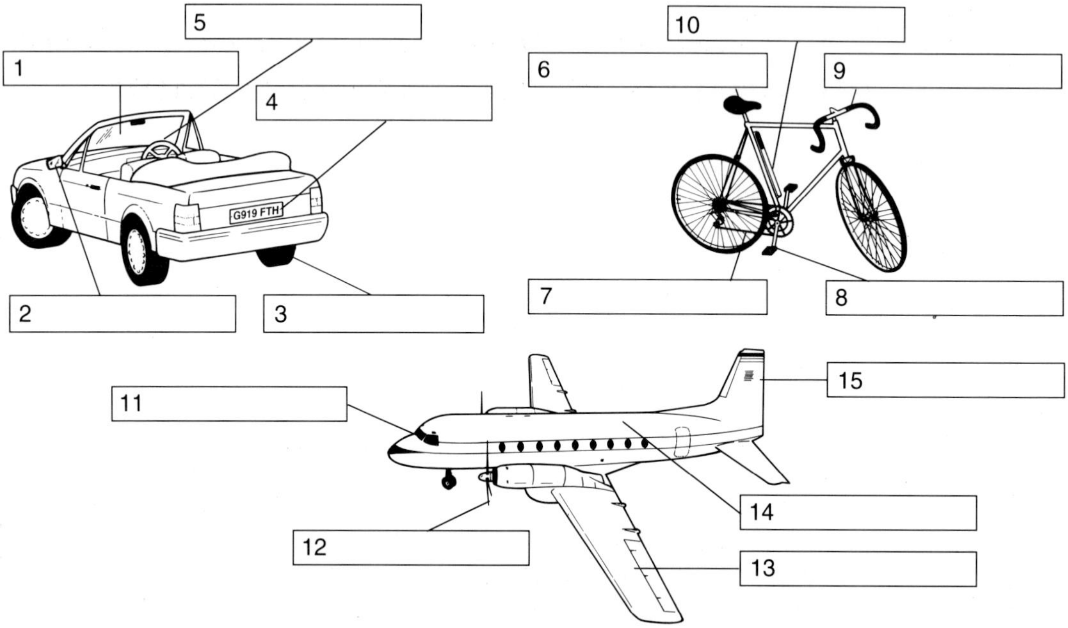

1
2
3
4
5
G919 FTH
6
7
8
9
10
11
12
13
14
15

2 Airport crossword

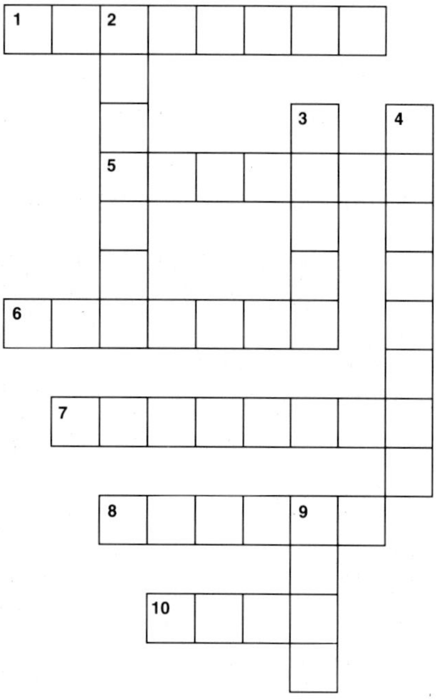

1
2
3
4
5
6
7
8
9
10

Across

1 ____ pass

5

6 ____ desk
(where you go to collect your *1 across*)

7

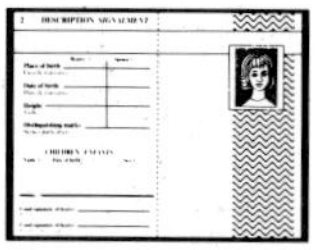

8 departure ____

10 You sit on this.

Down

2 ____ ticket

3 The part of the plane where the passengers are.

4 You can find an X-ray scanner here.

9 'Your flight is now boarding at ____ six.'

On Holiday Pages 71-73

Read the hotel information, look at the pictures, and fill in the missing words.

Sunnyview Hotel - information

Please leave your [1] _ _ _ _
_ _ _ at the hotel reception
when you go out.
Thank you.

Activities

Dalton Lake is only half a mile from the hotel. There you can go [2] _ _ _ _ _ _ _ or [3] _ _ _ _ _ _ _.

Northend-by-the-sea is a pretty holiday resort. Go [4] _ _ _ _ _ _ along the cliffs or just sit on the [5] _ _ _ _ _ and enjoy the sun!

If you want to do something really exciting, why not try [6] _ _ _ _ _ _ _ _ _ _ or even [7] _ _ _ _ - _ _ _ _ _ _ _?

SIGHTSEEING

Monday: Visit to Longleat, a historic [8] _ _ _ _ _ _ _ _ _ _ _ _ _ in Wiltshire.

Wednesday: A tour of the local countryside. A [9] _ _ _ _ _ _ is provided.

Friday: Coach trip to a beautiful [10] _ _ _ _ _ _ _ _ _.

Bring your camera!

1

2

3

4

5

6

7

8

9

10

Exercises page 137

Music and Theatre Pages 75-76

1 **Write the names of these instruments. The words are in the box, but the letters of each word have been mixed up.**

a

b
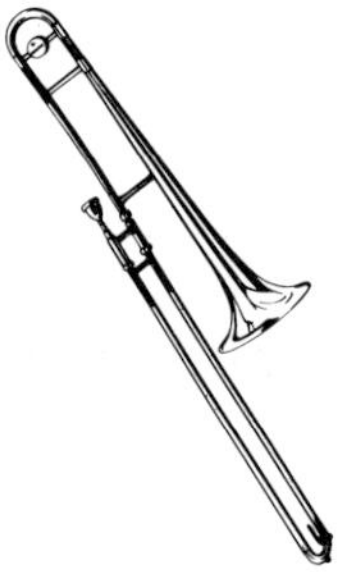

c
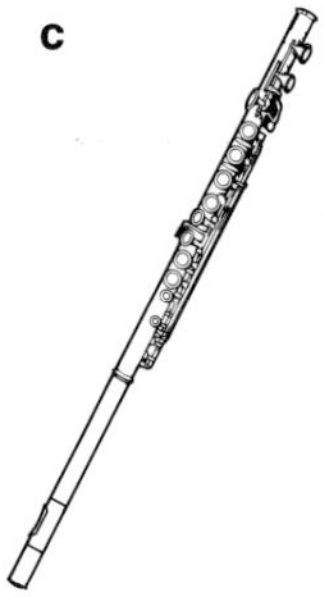

d
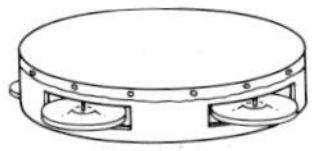

e

f

tufel	olcel
phosanoex	bornmote
beamotunir	slycbam

2 **What's the word?**

a You walk along this to get to your seat in a cinema or a theatre.

— — — — —

b He or she helps you to find your seat.

— — — — —

c Somebody who plays a large percussion instrument.

— — — — — — —

d Where the orchestra sits.

— — —

e The American word for a 'balcony' in a cinema or a theatre.

— — — — — — — — —

f Actors and actresses wait here before they go on stage.

— — — — —

g A word that means 'singer'.

— — — — — — — —

h Things on the stage of a theatre that make it look like a real place.

— — — — — — —

Now take the first letter of each of the words you found for **a**, **b** and **c**, the second letter of **d** and **e** and the third letter of **f**, **g** and **h**. You will then have the word for a group of people who are watching a film or a play!

____

Sports Pages 77-81

1 Fill in the table using words from the box.
Use each word only once.

Sport	Person	Place	Equipment
		court	
	caddy		
cricket			
		track	
			starting-gate

racket athlete jockey club horse-racing stumps starting-block golf field racecourse batsman tennis athletics umpire fairway

2 Sports Quiz

a Name three sports in which players **tackle** each other.

____

b What is the other name for **ping-pong**?

____

c Name three objects that you need for playing baseball.

____

d In which sport do players use **sticks**?

____

e Name a sport that takes place under water.

____

f Name three sports that need a **net**.

____

Exercises page 139

Verbs Pages 83-86

1 What shall I do now?

Bob never knows what to do. Give him some advice by writing the correct numbers by the letters.

a The kitchen window is really dirty.
g This newspaper is too big for my bag.
b What shall I do when the water boils?
f What shall I do with this candle?
c How do I open the door?
d This bag is too heavy to carry.
e I want to open this carton but I haven't got any scissors.

1 Why don't you put it down?
2 Light it!
3 Fold it!
4 Just push it!
5 You should clean it more often.
6 Try tearing it!
7 Pour it into the teapot!

a ______ b ______ c ______ d ______ e ______ f ______ g ______

2 Match these verbs to the right thing or person.

You can...

cook	a friend
brush	a glass
dig	the drive
hug	your hair
shake	dinner
sweep	hands
fill	the soil

Animals

Pages 89-93

Wordsnake

Complete the puzzle with the first letter of each word at the correct number. Every answer except the first begins with the last letter of the word before it.

1 An insect with hard wings.
2 A large grey animal with a trunk.
3 A wild animal with yellow fur and black stripes.
4 It's got a horn on its nose.
5 This small animal has got a big tail and lives in trees.
6 A reptile with a long body usually seen in hot, dry places.
7 A young one of these is called a puppy.
8 It has a very long neck.
9 It looks like a snake and lives in water.
10 A young sheep.
11 A large black animal with horns found mainly in Asia and Africa.
12 It has got eight 'arms'.
13 We get wool from these.
14 A large animal with black and white fur.
15 A very small insect.

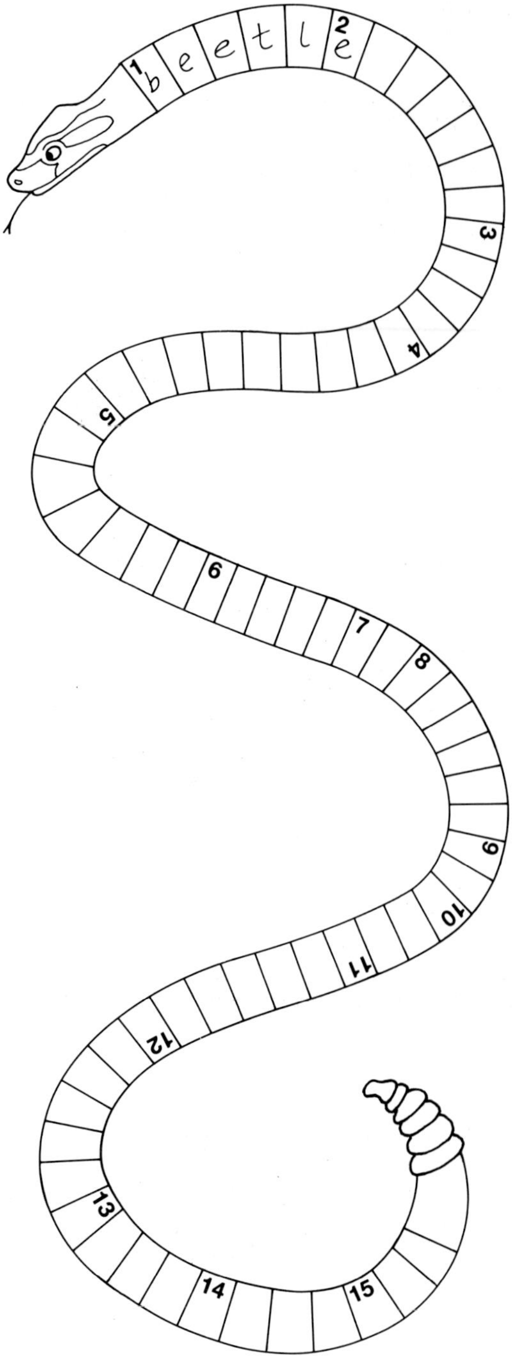
1
b e e t l
2
e
3
4
5
6
7
8
9
10
11
12
13
14
15

Key to exercises page 141

People and Health page 110

1
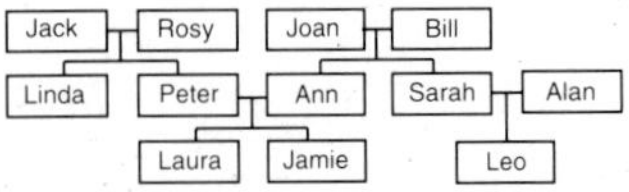

Jack
Rosy
Joan
Bill
Linda
Peter
Ann
Sarah
Alan
Laura
Jamie
Leo

2 ankle, back, cheek, chest, chin, eye, finger, fist, head, knee, lip, nail, neck, stomach, toe

3 **b** 1 **c** 4 **d** 5 **e** 2

Clothes page 111

1 **a** patterned, plain **b** striped, grey **c** polka-dot **d** pink, tartan

2 The girl is carrying an umbrella.
The woman is carrying a handbag and a briefcase.
The man is carrying a sweater.

3 belt - waist, watch - wrist, glove - hand, tights - legs, helmet - head, tie - neck

4 2. scarf 3. umbrella 4. purse 5. briefcase 6. earring 7. necklace 8. handbag 9. ring 10. shoelace 11. wallet 12. sun-glasses
dressing gown

At Home page 112

1 **a** freezer **b** scales **c** vase **d** oven **e** bush

2 **a** frying-pan **b** plate **c** rolling-pin **d** fork **e** ladle **f** kettle **g** jug **h** toaster

3 **a** *false.* The box of tissues is on the bedside cabinet. **b** *true.* **c** *false.* There's a hair-drier on the chest of drawers. **d** *false.* The dressing table is next to the chest of drawers. **e** *true.* **f** *false.* There's a poster between the light and the alarm clock.

Shopping and Food page 113

1 loaf of bread, bar of chocolate, bottle of mineral water, jar of jam, packet of biscuits, tub of margarine, box of cereal

2 1. bananas, punnet 2. flowers, irises 3. box, shelf, wrapping paper, reel 4. waiter, starter

3 1. market 2. florist's 3. newsagent's 4. restaurant

Dates and Times page 114

1 1. c, k 2. f, i 3. g, l 4. a, j 5. b,d 6. e, h

2 **a** On the sixteenth of April/ April the sixteenth. **b** On the first of May/ May the first. **c** On the third of August/ August the third. **d** On the twelfth of September/ September the twelfth. **e** On the thirtieth of November/ November the thirtieth.

At Work page 115

1 newsreader, travel agent, carpenter, baker, vet, mechanic

2 **a** hairdresser **b** lorry driver **c** pharmacist **d** disc jockey

3 desk, diary, disk, fax, file, letter, notebook, pen, print, screen, stapler, type

Describing Things page 116

1 **a** circle **b** square **c** rectangle **d** triangle **e** oval **f** cylinder

2 **a** 3 **b** 4 **c** 5 **d** 2 **e** 1 It's a **ruler**.

3 1. straight 2. thick 4. loose 5. full 6. solid 7. wet **shallow**

The Weather page 117

1
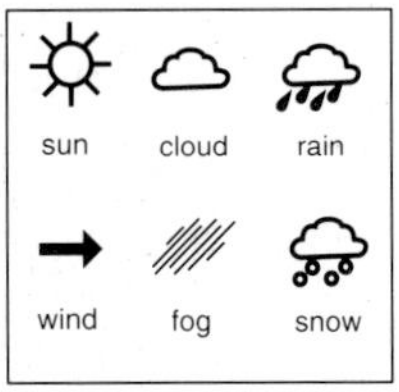

sun
cloud
rain
wind
fog
snow

windy snowy foggy rainy

2 1. cold 2. foggy 3. warm 4. sunny 5. cloudy 6. temperature 7. cool 8. rain 9. windy 10. minus 11. snow

The City page 118

1 mailbox, pavement, intersection, roundabout, litter-bin, crosswalk

2 **a** away from, road sign **b** across, road **c** into, building **d** along, pavement **e** towards, bus stop

Travelling page 119

1 1. windscreen 2. wing mirror 3. tyre 4. number-plate 5. steering-wheel 6. saddle 7. chain 8. pedal 9. handlebar 10. pump 11. cockpit 12. propeller 13. wing 14. fuselage 15. tail

2 1. boarding 2. airline 3. cabin 4. security 5. luggage 6. check-in 7. passport 8. lounge 9. gate 10. seat

On Holiday page 120

1. room key 2. sailing 3. fishing 4. hiking 5. beach 6. ballooning 7. hang-gliding 8. country house 9. picnic 10. waterfall

Music and Theatre page 121

1 **a** cello **b** trombone **c** flute **d** tambourine **e** saxophone **f** cymbals

2 **a** aisle **b** usher **c** drummer **d** pit **e** mezzanine **f** wings **g** vocalist **h** scenery **audience**

Sports page 122

1

Sport	*Person*	*Place*	*Equipment*
tennis	umpire	court	racket
golf	caddy	fairway	club
cricket	batsman	field	stumps
athletics	athlete	track	starting-block
horse-racing	jockey	racecourse	starting-gate

2 **a** rugby, hockey, football **b** table tennis **c** batting helmet, baseball glove/mitt, face mask/catcher's mask **d** hockey **e** scuba-diving **f** basketball, volleyball, badminton, *or* tennis

Verbs page 123

1 **a** 5 **b** 7 **c** 4 **d** 1 **e** 6 **f** 2 **g** 3

2 brush your hair, dig the soil, hug a friend, shake hands, sweep the drive, fill a glass

Animals page 124

1. beetle 2. elephant 3. tiger 4. rhinoceros 5. squirrel 6. lizard 7. dog 8. giraffe 9. eel 10. lamb 11. buffalo 12. octopus 13. sheep 14. panda 15. ant